The
LITURGICAL
MINISTRY
SERIES

GUIDE FOR LITURGY COMMITTEES

Paul Turner
Michael R. Prendergast

LTP

LITURGY
TRAINING
PUBLICATIONS

Psalm 22:26b–27, 28 and 30, 31–32

R. *I will praise you, Lord, in the assembly of your people.*

I will fulfill my vows before those who fear the LORD.
  The lowly shall eat their fill;
they who seek the LORD *shall praise him:*
  "May your hearts live forever!" R.

All the ends of the earth
  shall remember and turn to the LORD;
all the families of the nations
  shall bow down before him.

R. *I will praise you, Lord, in the assembly of your people.*

To him alone shall bow down
  all who sleep in the earth;
before him shall bend
  all who go down into the dust. R.

R. *I will praise you, Lord, in the assembly of your people.*

And to him my soul shall live;
  my descendants shall serve him.
Let the coming generation be told of the LORD
  that they may proclaim to a people yet to be born
  the justice he has shown. R.

R. *I will praise you, Lord, in the assembly of your people.*

Table of Contents

The ultimate goal for members of the liturgy committee should be to ensure that the assembly is led to that full, conscious, and active participation in the liturgy.

Preface

"Master, we have worked hard all night and have caught nothing, but at your command I will lower the nets."

—Luke 5:5

Simon had planned everything perfectly. Two boats rested at the shore. Andrew, James, and John were finishing dinner at their homes. They were gathering up stories and laughter, skills, and tools. Soon they would all rendezvous at the lake to do what they had practiced, performed, and enjoyed all their lives. They were going fishing.

Simon was bringing a new net. He was especially proud of it. Tight and strong, it seemed even more anxious for work than he was. He hoisted it like a trophy and shook it in triumph. "You'll have fresh fish for breakfast," he promised his wife. She smiled and kissed him. He strode out the door.

Simon was a natural leader. He provided for his family. He made friends easily. People respected his knowledge of the sea, his organizational skills, and his way with words. They gladly followed his directions, and they let him speak on their behalf.

Celebration filled the air as night fell on the waters. Simon and his companions leaped into the boats and pushed out into the deep. The moment had arrived. Simon got the attention of his friends; then he tossed his new net into the lake and hauled it back toward the boat.

Nothing. Andrew cocked an eyebrow. Simon shrugged and tossed again. John helped him pull the net back this time.

Nothing again. They both looked perplexed. Something was wrong. Just for the sheer novelty of the idea, they tossed the new net to the other side of the boat and hauled it in. Empty.

Simon sat down. The conversation became as still as the sea. Simon ran back through his mental checklist. He had planned everything just right: He brought his tools. He navigated to the right location. The proper hour for fishing had arrived. It was just odd.

"It has to work," he concluded. So he tossed the net again. And again. And again. And again. All night long, Simon and his friends worked as hard as they had ever worked. They had nothing to show for it—absolutely nothing but raw nerves and calloused hands.

Dawn broke. Simon parked his boat on the shore while the others kept trying. He simply could not believe he had failed. He cleaned his new net—not that it needed much attention. After that, he wanted to be alone—away from his friends—before going home.

Excited voices suddenly rose in the distance. Simon's moment of solitude was shattered by a crowd of villagers turning toward the lake. In his morning of embarrassment, Simon did not want an audience. But dozens of people descended upon him, all following a man heading toward the lake.

"Over here," he was saying. "There! There's a boat!" the stranger announced, grinning through his beard, and pointing toward Simon's newly abandoned craft. "Sir," the stranger said to Simon, "Mind if I use your boat?" He stepped in without awaiting a response.

"Lousy time for fishing," Simon said. "And you can't fit this many people in a skiff."

"No, no," the man explained. "I need a place to teach. Push this thing off a bit for me, would you?"

Andrew looked puzzled. Someone from the crowd filled him in: "This is Jesus. We've come to hear the word of God."

Simon was too tired to argue. Besides, he needed something to distract the crowd from his night of failure. He tipped the boat gently toward the water. Jesus sat down in it and spoke. The water amplified the sound of his voice, and everyone heard plainly. Simon had to respect a guy with organizational skills like that. It seemed as though this Jesus had no plan at all, yet he used the people, the tools, and even the landscape to his advantage. The man was a leader. He could speak well. People listened to him.

Simon was still lost in his thoughts when Jesus wrapped up his speech and turned his face toward the failed fisher. "Put out into deep water," he said to Simon. Then he called out to Andrew, James, and John, "and lower your nets for a catch!"[1]

This was too much. Simon was a professional fisher. This guy obviously was not. He was a smooth-tongued philosopher. Simon wanted to show respect, but he didn't need advice. He knew perfectly well how to fish. True, he had no fish at the moment to prove it, but this was his life. Besides, he would now have to admit his failure publicly. Simon tightened his lips and said to Jesus, "Master, we have worked hard all night and have caught nothing." Then, exhausted, trying to save face, he decided to teach the teacher a lesson. "But at your command I will lower the nets."[2]

Jesus smiled, sat back, hands behind his head, and watched.

Simon lifted his clean new net and tossed it into the lake. The water shook beneath the boat. Simon pulled on the net. It wouldn't budge. Andrew helped. Together they strained. To his horror, Simon noticed something. "My new net! It's breaking!" They signaled to their friends in the other boat. "Guys, get over here, would you?" It took the force of all of them to haul the fish on board. Sardines, musht, and catfish spilled all over the deck of Simon's boat, flopping in loud celebration and covering Jesus up to his hips.

The boat began to sink under the weight of the fish. Simon's net was torn, and now he was in danger of losing his boat. He fell to his knees, fish slapping at his thighs. He didn't feel like much of a leader, but he raised his voice above the din and gave Jesus a command. "Depart from me, Lord, for I am a sinful man."[3]

But Jesus had another plan. He spoke to the man who thought he had it all organized: his boat, his net, his friends, and his life. Jesus said something that caused Simon to give it all up at once: "Do not be afraid."[4]

Simon and his friends reached the shore, where they abandoned their boat and their nets, their skills and their know-how. They didn't need them anymore. They would no longer catch fish. They would catch people. Jesus had a plan. Now they had to prepare for it.

Paul Turner

NOTES

1. Luke 5:4.

2. Luke 5:5.

3. Luke 5:8.

4. Luke 5:10.

Welcome

A liturgy committee helps prepare a community to carry out the Church's plan of worship. The members represent different areas of expertise. They come to a meeting ready to put their knowledge and skills to work for the sake of others. As with any committee work, there is always a little give and take. Sometimes the members work hard and have little to show for it. Usually the results are not quite what any individual had in mind. The goal is to do what God has in mind. The goal is to discern the prompting of the Holy Spirit.

You are serving your community as a member of the liturgy committee. Your work is essential for the smooth execution of the complicated liturgies of the Roman Catholic Church. You will bring experience, energy, and ideas to your work. You will also bring a willing spirit that desires to do what is best for those with whom you worship.

About This Book

This book will help you understand the work of the liturgy committee, and where you and your skills fit. It will explain what the liturgy is about and how liturgy committees came to be. It will offer you spiritual reflection on the gifts God has given you, and it will answer your practical questions.

For work like this, many people arrive with a plan. They have experience at prayer—both private and communal. Sometimes they bring a new tool. They can envision different ways to enhance the community's worship. But when they open themselves to the word of God, they experience the presence of Jesus. It is he who teaches, he who inspires, and he who commands. Whenever our plan is not God's plan, we will be asked to abandon what we used to think is best. But that decision can bring new breath to discipleship, and new spirit to worship.

About the Authors

This book was written by two authors. Paul Turner wrote the first sections of the book, "Preface," "Theology and History of the Liturgy Committee," and "Spirituality and Formation of the Liturgy Committee Member." He is the pastor of Saint Munchin parish in Cameron, Missouri, and its mission, Saint Aloysius in Maysville. A priest of the diocese of Kansas City–St. Joseph, he holds a doctorate in sacred theology from Sant' Anselmo in Rome. He is the author of many pastoral resources about sacraments and the liturgy.

Michael R. Prendergast wrote "Serving on the Liturgy Committee," "Frequently Asked Questions," "Resources," "Glossary," and the appendixes. Michael has more than thirty years' experience as a musician and liturgist at the parish, cathedral, and diocesan levels. Michael is a freelance liturgical consultant, author, and pastoral musician who also serves as the coordinator of liturgy at Saint Andrew Parish in Portland, Oregon. For several years he served as the editor of *Today's Liturgy* at Oregon Catholic Press. He is the co-author, with William Belford and Glenn C. J. Byer, of *Parish Liturgy Basics* (Pastoral Press). Michael's most recent books are *Sunday Celebration in the Absence of a Priest, Revised Edition: A Pastoral Liturgical Commentary* (FDLC) and *The Song of the Assembly Pastoral Music in Practice: Essays in Honor of Father Virgil C. Funk*, editor with Bari Colombari, (Pastoral Press). Michael served on the Bishops' Committee on the Liturgy (BCL)[1] task force for the revision of the ritual book *Sunday Celebration in the Absence of a Priest* (USCCB, 2007).

Questions for Discussion and Reflection

1. Why have you agreed to serve on the liturgy committee at your church?

_____

_____

_____

_____

2. What do you hope to gain in your understanding of the theology and function of the ministry through this book?

_____

_____

_____

_____

NOTES

1. This committee is now known as the Bishops' Committee on Divine Worship (BCDW).

Theology and History of the Liturgy Committee

I received from the Lord what I also handed on to you. . . . As often as you eat this bread and drink the cup, you proclaim the death of the Lord until he comes.

—1 Corinthians 11:23, 26

Liturgical Prayer

A liturgy committee gives shape to the liturgy, but the liturgy gives shape to the committee members. To serve well requires a good understanding of what liturgy is, how it evolved, and how it stays fresh.

✠ For the liturgy, through which "the work of our redemption takes place," [Secret prayer of the Ninth Sunday after Pentecost] especially in the divine sacrifice of the Eucharist, is supremely effective in enabling the faithful to express in their lives and portray to others the mystery of Christ and the real nature of the true church.

—*Constitution on the Sacred Liturgy (CSL), 2*

The liturgy is the official prayer of the Church. Through Eucharist our redemption is accomplished, for when we eat and drink the body and blood of the Lord, we are already at table with Christ in the kingdom of heaven. Jesus promised that those who eat his body and drink his blood remain in him and he in them.[1] The liturgy benefits those who celebrate it.

The liturgy also benefits the world. Through it those who celebrate manifest the mystery of Christ to others. They live according to his teachings and in the life of his Holy Spirit. They also express what the Church is: a human and divine entity, active in the world with prayer and service, yet on pilgrimage to that city yet to come.[2]

4

Sunday Eucharist

Of all the things the Church does, nothing is more important than Sunday Eucharist. The liturgy is the source and summit of Christian faith. At the start of the week, Sunday Mass is the source of our strength. It is also the goal toward which our week strives. When we gather for Eucharist, we celebrate all that has been accomplished, and we receive nourishment to do God's will again in the days ahead.

> ✠ The liturgy is the summit toward which the activity of the church is directed; it is also the source from which all its power flows.
> —CSL, 10

The Church's mission requires the participation of everyone—both in worship and in prayer. The obligation pertaining to Mass on Sunday is not just to attend, but to participate.[3] The Church desires full, conscious, and active participation of the faithful at worship.

Your work on a liturgy committee, then, fulfills these aims. You will facilitate the participation of the people in the wondrous act of Eucharist. There, as we eat and drink the body and blood of the Lord, the work of our redemption is accomplished, we reach the summit of our activity as a Church, and we drink from the fount of the Spirit of Christ.

Of all the things the Church does, nothing is more important than Sunday Eucharist.

You will do this not just in your work, but in the attitude you bring to it. As you work in harmony with others, you are already demonstrating the Church at work: the body of Christ, the parts working together to glorify God and to serve others.

> ✠ It is very much the wish of the church that all the faithful should be led to take that full, conscious, and active part in liturgical celebrations which is demanded by the very nature of the liturgy, and to which the Christian people, "a chosen race, a royal priesthood, a holy nation, a redeemed people" (1 Pet. 2:9, 4–5) have a right and to which they are bound by reason of their Baptism.
> —CSL, 14

Ritual Prayer and Liturgical Law

✠ Among all who are involved with regard to the rites, pastoral aspects, and music there should be harmony and diligence in the effective preparation of each liturgical celebration in accord with the Missal and other liturgical books. This should take place under the rector of the church and after the consultation with the faithful about things that directly pertain to them.

—General Instruction of the Roman Missal (GIRM), 111

The liturgy of the Catholic Church is a stylized, ritual prayer. The Church promulgates detailed documents that steer this ritual. The basic format does not change, although significant components do, such as the biblical readings and the Eucharistic Prayer. The solid structure has fluid elements. Still, to a casual observer it may look repetitive and uninteresting. Only those who let the liturgy guide their prayer discover its richness.

Each celebration follows a prescribed set of actions and words. These have accumulated and evolved over the long history of the Church. When we perform the prayers and gestures of the liturgy, we repeat what generations of Catholics have done before us. We join with the Church past and present as we anticipate the joyous day of celebration in the future when we will participate fully at the divine liturgy of heaven.

The Church calendar for the liturgical year forms the setting for individual celebrations. The prayer texts for Mass have been carefully composed to draw out the meaning and spirit of seasons and feasts. Wherever you go around the Catholic world, the same prayers and actions are observed in one church after another. This practice stresses the universal nature of our Church, and it forms a global chorus of praise, offering sacrifice and service to God, through Jesus, in the Holy Spirit.

To accomplish this, the Church issues a series of liturgical documents that explain the liturgy and promote its careful celebration. The principal sources of these documents are the Holy See, the Conference of Bishops, and the diocesan Bishop.[4]

The liturgy of the Catholic Church is a stylized, ritual prayer. Pictured here is the Entrance Procession at Mass.

The Holy See is also called the Apostolic See. It is the administrative arm of the Roman Catholic Church, and it includes the Pope and the various congregations of the curia.[5] In liturgical matters, the Pope relies upon the Sacred Congregation for Divine Worship and the Discipline of the Sacraments. As with all congregations, a cardinal is placed in charge of its work. The Apostolic See publishes the liturgical books containing the rites of the Roman Catholic Church. As with all universal communication from the Vatican, the first language of publication is Latin. The Apostolic See reviews and approves the vernacular translations of these texts. The English translations are submitted by the International Commission on English in the Liturgy, a group of bishops representing 11 different conferences, who maintain a common secretariat in Washington, DC. The congregation consults another committee called Vox Clara about translations into English. The Holy See also safeguards the faithful observance of liturgical regulations.[6]

Examples of significant publications from the Holy See include the Roman Missal, together with its *General Instruction*, all of the ritual books from the *Rite of Christian Initiation of Adults* to the *Order of Christian Funerals*, as well as the legislation governing vernacular translations, such as *Liturgiam authenticam*.

A Conference of Bishops is a regional entity, usually formed by the bishops of a particular country. The United States Conference of Catholic Bishops assumes this function in the United States. The primary liturgical responsibility of the conference is the preparation and publication of vernacular translations of the liturgy.[7] The liturgical books authorize the conferences to make some adaptations to the rites, and these adaptations are also included in the respective vernacular translations.[8]

For example, when the revised *General Instruction of the Roman Missal* was promulgated in Latin in 2000, the bishops of the United States incorporated several adaptations, many of them already being observed, such as a lengthening of the time when the faithful kneel at Mass.[9] Earlier, the conference omitted the use of the oil of catechumens at the Easter Vigil.[10] It has the authority to make more specific and detailed formularies of the renunciations that precede the profession of faith at Baptism, though this has never been done in the United States.[11] The same conference has issued guidelines for art and architecture in Catholic churches.[12]

The diocesan Bishop is the director, promoter, and guardian of the liturgical life in the Church entrusted to him.[13] He may administer policies for the diocese or intervene in singular instances.[14] He may not act contrary to a higher law.[15] The *praenotanda* (foreword/pastoral introduction) of many liturgical books assigns the Bishop specific authority concerning some elements of the celebrations. The Bishop directs a diocesan commission that promotes the liturgical apostolate.[16]

A Bishop may publish diocesan directives concerning the liturgy. For example, he may expand the occasions for Holy Communion under both forms.[17] He may authorize congregations in the United States to remain standing at Mass after the Lamb of God.[18] For a serious reason he may also dispense the elect from participating in one or more of the three scrutinies preceding their initiation.[19]

Liturgical law comes from various sources. Universal legislation is found in the liturgical books, the *Code of Canon Law*,[20] and pronouncements on the liturgy from the Holy See.[21] Some of these statements have more to do with theology and pastoral care than they do with law. For example, the Pope may issue letters or exhortations in this vein. But when he writes an apostolic constitution, he issues a most solemn form of papal legislation. Pope Paul VI's apostolic constitution for the sacrament of Confirmation, for example, changed the formula used by a Bishop to administer the sacrament. The Pope may also issue legislation under the form of *motu proprio*, or "under his own initiative," as John Paul II did in 2002 when he promoted individual confession of sins and specified the restrictions for communal confession and absolution.[22]

Dicasteries,[23] such as the Sacred Congregation for Divine Worship and the Discipline of the Sacraments, do not issue laws or general decrees unless the Pope specifically approves such an action in an individual case.[24] A general decree by the congregation must cite that approval, and it cannot revoke previous legislation.[25] Examples pertaining to the liturgy include *Liturgiam authenticam*, which regulates the translation of Latin liturgical texts into the vernacular languages; *Redemptionis sacramentum*, which addressed a number of liturgical abuses; the *Directory for Masses with Children*, which permits some adjustments at Mass to enhance the way children appreciate the liturgy; and the *Directory for the Application of Principles and Norms on Ecumenism*, which guides the observance of worship between Catholics and other Christians.

Additional norms may be established by the Conference of Bishops, the diocesan Bishop, the vicar general and episcopal vicar. A policy established by a diocesan worship office has force only with an express mandate from the Bishop or competent vicar. Such law is commonly issued in a statement called a directory. Other documents may be called declarations, norms, or letters.[26]

There is some variation in the weight of these documents, depending on who issues them and why. But all the directives of the Church deserve a charitable and open hearing, as well as a devout intention to carry them out.

The Second Vatican Council established guidelines for liturgical adaptation.[27] The faithful around the world received news of this theme with warmth and enthusiasm.

Some adaptations are assigned to the Conference of Bishops. These are generally found in the introductory material to the liturgical books. Others are given to the diocesan Bishop. And some are given to the minister. These usually consist of a choice of texts for the sake of the people,[28] or in cases where he is given a sample text and allowed to use "these or similar words." When making these choices, the priest should have the common spiritual good in mind, not his personal preference.[29] More profound adaptations may be made, especially in mission territories, with the approval of the Apostolic See.[30]

> ✠ Even in the liturgy the church does not wish to impose a rigid uniformity in matters which do not affect the faith or the well-being of the entire community. Rather does it cultivate and foster the qualities and talents of the various races and nations. Anything in people's ways of life which is not indissolubly bound up with superstition and error the church studies with sympathy, and, if possible, preserves intact. It sometimes even admits such things into the liturgy itself, provided that they harmonize with its true and authentic spirit.
> —*CSL, 37*

Sometimes a norm is established through custom rather than law. In this case, the longstanding custom of a particular community becomes its norm. Customs may obtain the force of law after 30 years of continuous observance.[31]

Some adaptations to the liturgy may and should happen. Ordinarily, however, it is best to know the universal and local liturgical laws, and to let them guide the work of a liturgy committee. The two books you will want to know the best are the Roman Missal (formerly called the Sacramentary) and the *Lectionary for Mass.*

The rules and regulations for liturgy are meant to ensure its smooth execution. They hope to deepen the community's experience of prayer. Some people are put off by liturgical law on the grounds that it stifles the Spirit, but it is meant to enliven the Spirit on a different level. You never grow tired of your favorite music. You get something more out of a favorite book every time you read it. You return to a certain body of water, a spectacular view, or a special building time and again because it renews you every time you experience it. The same is true for liturgical prayer. The more we enter it, the more it speaks to us.

Planning or Preparing?

Because of the nature of Catholic worship, it may be better to think of your role as preparing the liturgy, rather than planning it.[32] You don't plan for Mass the way you plan a meal, deciding what food to use and how to prepare it. Rather, you prepare the Mass the way you prepare food from a good recipe. You know the formula, but now you make it. You use the guidelines together with your own creativity, spirit, and experience.

Even so, preparing is only one step. People will celebrate the liturgy you helped prepare, and then they will think about it. Members of the liturgy committee will evaluate the ministers, the music, and the success of their preparations for individual days and entire liturgical seasons. With these insights, they will make better preparations in the future.

You are most familiar with your own role when you come to worship. But on the committee it will be good for you to become familiar with as many liturgical ministries as you can.

Members of the liturgy committee should be familiar with the various liturgical roles. Pictured here is the cantor and priest celebrant during the Liturgy of the Eucharist.

PRIEST: The priest is called the celebrant of the liturgy. He stands "at the head of the faithful people gathered together here and now, presides over their prayer, proclaims the message of salvation to them, associates the people with himself in the offering of sacrifice through Christ in the Holy Spirit to God the Father, gives his brothers and sisters the Bread of eternal life, and partakes of it with them."[33] He should do this with dignity and humility.

DEACON: The deacon assists the priest in the orderly celebration of Eucharist. "At Mass the deacon has his own part in proclaiming the Gospel, in preaching God's word from time to time, in announcing the intentions of the Prayer of the Faithful, in ministering to the priest, in preparing the altar and serving the celebration of the Sacrifice, in distributing the Eucharist to the faithful, especially under the species of wine, and sometimes in giving directions regarding the people's gestures and posture."[34]

THE PEOPLE: Those who assemble as the congregation express their identity as the holy people of God, "a people whom God has made his own, a royal priesthood, so that they may give thanks to God and offer the spotless Victim not only through the hands of the priest but also together with him, and so that they may learn to offer themselves."[35]

ACOLYTES AND SERVERS: These ministers "serve at the altar and assist the priest and the deacon; they may carry the cross, the candles, the thurible, the bread, the wine, and the water, and they may also be deputed to distribute Holy Communion as extraordinary ministers."[36]

LECTORS: Lectors proclaim the readings from Sacred Scripture, except for the Gospel. They may lead the Prayer of the Faithful and read the psalm if it is not sung.[37]

MUSICIANS: The choir, the cantor, the psalmist, and instrumentalists all contribute to the singing at Mass. They carry out the parts assigned to them and foster "the active participation of the faithful through the singing."[38]

SACRISTAN: The sacristan "carefully arranges the liturgical books, the vestments, and other things necessary in the celebration of Mass."[39]

OTHER MINISTERS: Other people carry out additional functions: those who greet at the door, those who take up the collection, those who bring forward the gifts, those who offer childcare, and those who set the liturgical environment with the tasteful use of art, flowers, and other items for the delight of the eyes. No one is expert at everything that needs to be done. Instead, the Holy Spirit has dispersed gifts throughout the community. The gathering of these many gifts shows the diversity of the Holy Spirit and the life of the community that has received them in order to share them among the people of God.

Good liturgy is any liturgy in which people use these gifts. They praise God as best as they are able. You do not have to have the most skilled musicians or the most expressive lector. You do not need the best homilist or the strongest congregational singing. It matters that everyone comes ready to render thanks to God, using the gifts of the Spirit with the measure in which they are bestowed. Too many people evaluate liturgy based on what they got out of it. That isn't the point. The point is what *God* gets out of it. God deserves our full attention, the abandonment of our other concerns, and the devotion of our thoughts and deeds to him.

Questions for Discussion and Reflection

1. What is your role in the liturgy?

_____

_____

_____

2. How do you prepare yourself to celebrate liturgy?

_____

_____

_____

3. Name a "good liturgy" that you experienced recently. What made it special? Did something happen to you as a result of the experience?

_____

_____

_____

4. What areas of the Church's liturgical law do you wish you knew better? What steps can you take to learn more?

_____

_____

_____

Historical Roots

There has always been a need to prepare for the liturgy, but the need intensified after the Second Vatican Council. From the earliest days of worship, somebody always had to prepare the scriptures, the prayers, the bread and wine for the day's celebration. In the centuries following the Council of Trent (1545–1563), the Church further centralized many functions and the liturgy solidified into a predictable pattern. Celebrated in a common language (Latin), following a universal book of texts (the Roman Missal), the Mass seemed to be a simple matter to the casual observer. But its proper execution demanded the skills of language, posture, and ritual.

Second Vatican Council

The Second Vatican Council (1962–1965) introduced changes to the liturgy for the spiritual welfare of Christians everywhere:

> It is the wish of the church to undertake a careful general reform of the liturgy in order that the Christian people may be more certain to derive an abundance of graces from it. For the liturgy is made up of unchangeable elements divinely instituted, and of elements subject to change. These latter not only may be changed but ought to be changed with the passage of time, if they have suffered from the intrusion of anything out of harmony with the inner nature of the liturgy or have become less suitable. In this renewal, both texts and rites should be ordered so as to express more clearly the holy things by which they signify. The Christian people, as far as is possible, should be able to understand them easily and take

part in them in a celebration which is full, active and the community's own.[40]

> ✠ For the liturgy is made up of unchangeable elements divinely instituted, and of elements subject to change.
>
> —*CSL, 21*

The most notable of the changes were in language and posture. The Council permitted the use of vernacular languages in the liturgy, and the priest was allowed to face the people throughout the Mass, instead of having his back to them for most of it.

However, there were other extensive changes. The faithful used to participate in silence by following a missal or praying a Rosary. Now they participate through dialogues, song, and action. The Lectionary has been expanded tremendously. Previously only 1% of the Old Testament and 17% of the New Testament were included at the Mass each year. Today, over a three-year cycle, the faithful will hear 14% of the Old Testament and 71% of the New.[41] Formerly, every Mass used the same Eucharistic Prayer, but now the priest may choose from options. A wider variety of prefaces and other presidential prayers became available.

With these changes opened up a new treasury of liturgical music. The Gregorian chant that characterized the earlier liturgy remains a precious gem in the crown of Church music—in the crown of any music in history, for that matter. Now congregations are singing a broader repertoire of music, expressing a fuller range of Catholic beliefs in idioms that resonate with the times and regions of those who sing.

The number of ministers at Mass has grown. Lay ministers have been assigned to some parts of the service, and women have exercised more central roles in the liturgy than in the past—for example, by proclaiming the scriptures and assisting in the distribution of Holy Communion.

All these changes added new life to the Church's worship. But they came with a price. The liturgy required more preparation. A greater number of people had to be selected, trained, and evaluated. The choice of certain texts had to be made. For this reason, many parishes developed liturgy committees. These were inspired by the council's call for such committees among episcopal conferences and within dioceses. The complexities of the revised liturgy needed more attention, Catholics were enthusiastic about the coming developments, and committees formed in parishes to help implement the new universal norms.

Over the years since the council, liturgy committees have undergone some evolution. As people became more familiar with the revisions, they became more practiced at the art of preparing for Mass and other rites. The Vatican continues to release revised liturgical legislation, and the success of these norms requires skilled members of liturgy committees who will discover, read, embrace, and implement them to improve the experience of local worship.

Questions for Discussion and Reflection

1. What has been your experience with liturgy committees?

_____

_____

_____

_____

2. How has your participation at Mass changed in your lifetime?

_____

_____

_____

_____

NOTES

1. See John 6:56.

2. See *Constitution on the Sacred Liturgy* (CSL), 2; Hebrews 13:14.

3. See *Code of Canon Law*, 1247, 1248.

4. See John Huels, *Liturgy and Law: Liturgical Law in the System of Roman Catholic Canon Law* (Montréal: Wilson & Lafleur, 2006), pp. 39–56.

5. See canon 361.

6. Canon 838 §2.

7. See canon 838 §3.

8. Ibid.

9. See *General Instruction of the Roman Missal* (GIRM), 43.

10. See RCIA, 33 §7.

11. See RCIA, 33 §8.

12. See *Built of Living Stones: Art, Architecture and Worship* (BLS).

13. See canon 835 §1.

14. Canon 392 §2.

15. See canon 135 §2.

16. See CSL, 45.

17. See GIRM, 283.

18. See GIRM, 43.

19. See RCIA, 34 §3.

20. See especially Book IV.

21. See Huels, pp. 83–91.

22. See *Misericordia Dei*.

23. Dicasteries are departments of the Roman Curia.

24. See *Pastor bonus*, 18.

25. See canon 33 §1.

26. See Huels, pp. 88–89.

27. See Huels, pp. 119–43.

28. See GIRM, 24, 352.

29. See GIRM, 352.

30. For a thorough study of adaptations, see Kenneth J. Martin, *The Forgotten Instruction: The Roman Liturgy, Inculturation, and Legitimate Adaptations* (LTP, 2007).

31. See canons 23–28.

32. See Austin H. Fleming, Victoria M. Tufano, *Preparing for Liturgy: A Theology and Spirituality* (LTP, 1997).

33. GIRM, 93.

34. GIRM, 94.

35. GIRM, 95.

36. GIRM, 100.

37. See GIRM, 99, 101.

38. GIRM, 103. See also 102, 104.

39. GIRM, 105a.

40. CSL, 21.

41. Percentages obtained from "Nine Questions on the Ordinary and Extraordinary Forms of the *Missale Romanum,*" *NewsLetter: Committee on the Liturgy* XLIII (May/June 2007): 27.

Spirituality and Formation of the Liturgy Committee

> *Let your Spirit enlighten their minds / and guide all their actions / that they may be renewed in faith, / united in love, / and bring to fulfillment the work of your Church / to your greater honor and glory.*
>
> —Book of Blessings, 1902

Personal Rituals

When you serve on a liturgy committee you can more dramatically catch the vision of the entire liturgical year, the expanse of liturgical celebrations in the Church's repertoire of prayer, and the details of the rites that accent the journey of individual Catholics from their initiation, through their moments of passage, and on to their final rest. At the most and least significant times in the lives of individuals and communities, the Church is there. We bring centuries of experience to our rituals. We help people drink from the deep waters of our tradition.

In your own life, you find ways to acknowledge special seasons and occasions. You do some of this already. As a preliminary exercise for this section, take a moment to think about the rituals in your life.

BIRTHDAYS: How do you celebrate your birthday? What traditions do you observe when a family member or close friend has a birthday?

THANKSGIVING: Where do you go for the Thanksgiving meal? Who is there? What food is always there? How does your family relax and play together on this day?

ANNIVERSARIES: If you are married, how do you celebrate your anniversary? If you have lost a close relative or friend, do you observe the anniversary of death each year? How? If you are in religious life, how do you recognize the anniversary of your ordination or profession?

CHRISTMAS: How do you celebrate Christmas? How early do you begin? When do you decorate the house? When do you start wearing holiday clothes? When do you send out Christmas cards? After Christmas Day, how long do you leave up your tree? When do you take down the other decorations? How does your celebration of Christmas Day extend throughout the Christmas season of the liturgical year?

GOOD FRIDAY: Do you have any traditions for Good Friday? How do you remember the death of the Lord Jesus?

PERSONAL OBSERVANCES: Is there some day you always remember each year? It may be the anniversary of something tragic or something wonderful. Give an example of a day that is on your personal calendar each year. What rituals do you observe?

EVERY MORNING: You probably go through a set routine every morning without even thinking about it. You wake up. You prepare your body for the day. You select your clothes. You pray. You eat. What is your routine? What is your morning ritual? Why do you do these things? If one or more of them didn't happen, would your morning feel complete? Would it affect the rest of your day? How?

Religious Rituals

Every human being observes ritual practices. In the Catholic Church we formalize these as a community in our liturgical calendar. You already know the value of Sunday Mass. Perhaps you pray all or part of the Liturgy of the Hours as your daily prayer. In any event, you have adopted the liturgy as the anchor of your spiritual life.

You may have other devotions. You may enjoy reading at random from the Bible. You may pray the Rosary. You may say the chaplet of Divine Mercy. All these are worthy practices. But the liturgy of the Church is something special. The more you pray with the Mass, the Liturgy of the Hours, and the sacraments, the more your own heart beats with the central tradition of the Roman Catholic Church.

To help you in your spiritual life, here are some specific exercises you can do at different seasons of the year. They are here to help you observe the seasons, but also to familiarize yourself with the Church's liturgical books. The texts that focus your prayer in these exercises are not printed in this book. You will need to locate another book to work each exercise. This will help you know the main liturgical library of the Church, give you ways to reflect on your ministry, and prepare you for ways to pray with the Church's liturgy every day of your life.

Advent

Locate the first volume of the *Lectionary for Mass*. The Lectionary is in four volumes. The second and third are for daily Masses. The last volume is for the Church's sacraments and other needs and occasions. The first volume contains the readings for Sunday Mass. You will find the seasons of the year near the front of this volume. Ordinary Time takes up most of the rest of the book.

Start at the beginning with the season of Advent. Figure out which year of the Lectionary cycle you are in. If the calendar year that will begin on January 1 is divisible evenly by 3, you are in Year C of the cycle. When you divide by 3, if you have 1 left over, it's Year A; 2 left over is B. You can do this even more quickly by adding the four digits of the year and dividing that sum by 3. For example: 2 + 0 + 0 + 8 = 10; when you divide 10 by 3, you get 3 with 1 left over. The year 2008 was Year A, which began in Advent of 2007.

Not to digress, but the weekday readings are on a two-year cycle. The odd-numbered years are Year I. So 2008, beginning in Advent of 2007, was Year II for weekdays.

Find the four Sundays of Advent for this year. Now slowly, prayerfully, read through each of the second readings of the season. In general, these readings look forward to the Second Coming of Christ. Study each reading in turn, and ask yourself why it was chosen for the season of Advent. Look for words such as *coming* or statements that give reasons for hope. Then ask yourself the following questions.

Questions for Reflection

1. Why am I looking forward to the Second Coming of Christ?

_____

_____

_____

_____

2. What will he bring me that I lack right now?

_____

_____

_____

_____

3. What am I really longing for this Advent?

_____

_____

_____

_____

4. Am I longing for a particular Christmas gift, or am I really longing for something deeper? For the attention of someone? Or of some One?

_____

_____

_____

_____

Christmas

Get a copy of the *Sacramentary Supplement* and look for the Christmas Proclamation. (This is not in the Sacramentary, but in a separately published supplement.) This optional text may be sung at Midnight Mass just before the Gloria, in order to announce the birth of Christ. Even if your parish does not use it in the liturgy, it makes a wonderful text for meditation on the real meaning of Christmas.

The Christmas Proclamation announces the birth of Jesus within the framework of history. Notice the historical events that serve as benchmarks leading up to the first Christmas Day: the creation of the world, the flood of Noah, the covenant with Abraham, the Exodus from Egypt, the time of the judges, the anointing of David, the prophecy of Daniel—even the number of the olympiad and the founding of the city of Rome. The events pertain to religion, sports, and politics. The proclamation of Christmas Day announces that Jesus was born in time, but that he is Lord over all human activity and yearning.

Questions for Reflection

1. What have been ten significant moments in your life?

_____

_____

_____

_____

2. How many years is it now since each of them happened?

_____

_____

_____

_____

3. How would you group these moments?

_____

_____

_____

_____

4. Jesus is coming into your life this Christmas. He is Lord of all. How is he Lord of all in your life this year?

_____

_____

_____

_____

Ordinary Time during Winter

Between the Christmas season and the start of Lent, we celebrate several weeks of Ordinary Time. The number of weeks differs each year because the date of Easter varies so much. An early Easter makes a short space of Ordinary Time during the winter months. A late Easter makes it longer.

Each year, Ordinary Time during winter has this in common: For several weeks the Second Reading at Mass comes from 1 Corinthians. The early chapters appear in Year A of the cycle and the last ones are proclaimed in Year C. Each year we hear several key passages from this lengthy and important letter.

Open up Volume I of the _Lectionary for Mass_ and look for the Second Sunday in Ordinary Time. The readings begin at number 64. You'll find the readings of Years A, B, and C altogether before the Lectionary gives you the suite of readings for all three years of the Third Sunday in Ordinary Time. Look up the readings for this liturgical year. Flip ahead and find out how many weeks you'll be hearing from 1 Corinthians. Remember, to find this year's readings, you need to look past the other two years of the cycle.

The city of Corinth, whose citizens received this letter, is located on the isthmus that connects the two parts of the peninsula of Greece. It is a true crossroads. In Paul's day, it had its share of problems. The new Christian community was splintered by factions, and the faithful needed directions on everything from celebrating Eucharist to observing charity, to the meaning of the Resurrection.

Questions for Reflection

1. Study this year's readings from Paul's first letter to the Corinthians. What is he saying?

_____

_____

_____

_____

2. Which passages are most familiar to you?

_____

_____

_____

_____

3. How is Paul speaking to you right now?

_____

_____

_____

_____

4. How is Paul challenging you to be more faithful? What animosities is he asking you to put aside?

_____

_____

_____

_____

Lent

Use Volume I of the Lectionary again. Find the readings for the Sundays of Lent. They begin at number 22. Figure out which year of the cycle we are in. This time, study the first readings of Lent for the first five Sundays of the season. Each year the first readings walk you through a series of significant events in salvation history. You'll read excerpts from the historical and prophetic books of the Bible.

Questions for Reflection

1. Which highlights of salvation history are we remembering this year? Why?

_____

_____

_____

_____

2. What significance do they have for the elect and for the faithful?

_____

_____

_____

_____

3. What significance do these events have for you?

_____

_____

_____

4. What sin are you trying to overcome this year?

_____

_____

_____

5. How are these readings helping you face the challenge? Do they offer hope? How?

_____

_____

_____

_____

The Paschal Triduum

The Paschal Triduum is the hinge of the entire liturgical year. Easter ranks atop the list of solemnities in the Church's calendar, even though society gives much more attention to Christmas—for a variety of reasons. Easter celebrates the Resurrection of Jesus and our belief that we will rise again with him. It is the feast of our redemption.

Open the Sacramentary (or the Roman Missal) and turn to the Easter Vigil. There, near the beginning of the celebration, you will find the text for the Easter Proclamation, also known by its Latin name, the *Exsultet*. Fire is the primary symbol of the first part of the Vigil, and the lighting of the Paschal candle sets the stage for the singing of the *Exsultet*.

Read through this proclamation. Notice how it keeps repeating the importance of "this" night even when it speaks about events in history. It is as though history is collapsed into this very Easter night of this year. Heaven is wedded to earth, and we experience time as God does—all at once.

Questions for Reflection

1. What are you going to celebrate at this Easter Vigil?

---

2. How is Christ risen within you now?

---

3. How have you experienced death and Resurrection this Lent? How has the promise of new life come to you? What does *this* night mean for you?

---

4. This year, when have you crossed a Red Sea, leaving sin behind and finding grace on a new shore?

_____

_____

_____

_____

5. Is this the night when Christ is present to you again in that miracle of love?

_____

_____

_____

_____

6. As you ask God to accept the Paschal candle, what praise are you offering this Easter?

_____

_____

_____

_____

Ordinary Time during Summer and Fall

Choose at random four weeks of Ordinary Time later this year. Flip the first volume of the Lectionary open in the middle someplace and start there. Find four consecutive Sundays for this liturgical year. Read through the responsorial psalms.

As you read the psalms, notice the refrain. Pay attention to which verses of each psalm are being used. Only rarely do we sing an entire psalm as the responsory. Usually it's just a few verses. Sometimes the Responsorial Psalm is not really a psalm but rather a canticle from the Old or New Testament.

Ordinarily the psalm is chosen because it matches a theme established by the Gospel and the First Reading. Take a closer look at the sequence of readings on each of these four Sundays.

Questions for Reflection

1. Can you figure out why this particular psalm is an appropriate choice?

_____

_____

_____

_____

2. Why does the refrain work?

_____

_____

_____

_____

3. Why are these particular verses chosen for this week?

_____

_____

_____

_____

4. What is the link between the Responsorial Psalm and the other readings of the day?

_____

_____

_____

_____

Now pray the refrain. Pray it several times, like a mantra. For a moment forget about all the logical connections to the other readings, and just let the refrain of the psalm work on you. Let it become your prayer.

Repeat this exercise with all four psalms you have chosen. Select one refrain to use as a repeated prayer throughout the day.

Weddings

If you are involved with weddings, you know that they are frustrating and wonderful at the same time. Some liturgical ministers resent offering assistance at weddings, but these celebrations mark the start of a new family, and the Church has a special interest in their success. Before you pray with some of the texts for the wedding, get in touch with your own feelings about these celebrations.

Questions for Reflection

1. Are you happy to be part of weddings?

_____

_____

_____

_____

2. Do you look forward to them? If not, why not?

_____

_____

_____

_____

3. What parts of the wedding make it difficult for you to pray? What parts help you rejoice?

_____

_____

_____

_____

Think about some model couples in your life. Remember that they too had a wedding day. If you could have been present for their wedding, knowing what you now know about them, what spirit would you have brought to that ceremony?

Now get a copy of the *Rite of Marriage*. There will be one in the sacristy of your church. Look for the nuptial blessings. There are several, located at numbers 33, 120, and 121. In the second edition of the *Rite of Marriage* the numbers will be 74, 242, and 244.[1] Read through these texts prayerfully.

Questions for Reflection

1. The nuptial blessings give praise to God. For what do they praise God?

_____

_____

_____

_____

2. They are asking a particular favor for the couple. What are they requesting?

_____

_____

_____

_____

3. When you prepare for a wedding, for what do you praise God?

_____

_____

_____

_____

4. What are you asking God for this couple? How do you best express your care for them?

_____

_____

_____

_____

Funeral Mass

The funeral Mass is one of the great blessings our Church offers to the memory of the deceased and gives support to a grieving family. When people feel lost, not knowing where to turn, this ritual of the Church generally provides great comfort. Mourners need a process to help them come to grips with the death of someone they loved, to express their affection, and to provide a dignified interment.

People hear a lot of words at a funeral Mass. The funeral prayers of the Church—as with other liturgical prayers—have been formulated over centuries of experience. They quite often capture the very essence of loss and hope.

Use the Sacramentary (or Roman Missal) for this prayer experience. Look up the prefaces for funerals. The collection of prefaces is near the middle of the book, and the ones for funerals are at the end of the set.

Read through these prefaces (P77–80). They all praise God for something.

Questions for Reflection

The following questions may be used for group discussion or personal reflection concerning our role on a liturgy committee.

1. What are the prefaces saying? What do they articulate about our faith?

   _____

   _____

   _____

   _____

2. List the names of five of your family or friends who have died. Recalling your own grief, which of these prefaces would have spoken to you in each instance? Why?

   _____

   _____

   _____

   _____

Questions for Discussion and Reflection

1. What is your prayer routine? How do you pray every day? How do you pray on Sundays? How do you adjust your prayer to fit the seasons of the year?

   _____

   _____

   _____

   _____

2. How are you feeling challenged by your work on the liturgy committee? Is it through some areas of liturgical life unknown to you? Is it because of some of the people with whom you will serve?

_____

_____

_____

_____

3. What will you do to enrich your prayer life while you serve on this committee? How will you become more attentive to common liturgical prayer?

_____

_____

_____

_____

O God, the source of all graces,
  you sent your Holy Spirit onto your Church
  to bestow the gifts we would need.
Open our hearts to receive these gifts
  and to recognize them in one another.
Send your Holy Spirit here to help us pray
  and to lead others into your presence.
We ask this through Christ our Lord.
Amen.

NOTES

1. At the time of publication, the English translation of the second edition of the *Rite of Marriage* was still in preparation.

Serving on the
Liturgy Committee

Lord, / may everything we do / begin with your inspiration / and continue with your help, / so that all our prayers and works / may begin in you / and by you be happily ended.

—Book of Blessings, 552.B

The Pastoral or Parish Council

A pastoral or parish council is a collaborative body of the Christian faithful whose purpose is the promotion of the mission of Jesus Christ and the Church. The pastoral council works in close partnership with the pastor or pastoral administrator of the parish, advising these leaders in matters pertaining to pastoral ministry: to identify, implement, and evaluate those pastoral preparations and policies best suited to expand the Gospel of Jesus Christ.[1]

A pastoral council may be established in every parish or cluster of parishes.[2] The norms for pastoral councils may vary from place to place, but it is the responsibility of the diocesan Bishop to provide direction and oversee the implementation and structure of pastoral councils within the diocese.

Typically, a pastoral council may

- act as a policy formulating body in all matters of pastoral ministry of the parish except those already established by the local diocese;

- include representatives from the parish finance council, liturgical

✠ If the diocesan bishop judges it opportune . . . a pastoral council is to be established in each parish, over which the pastor presides and in which the Christian faithful, together with those who share in pastoral care by virtue of their office in the parish, assist in fostering pastoral activity.

A pastoral council possesses a consultative vote only and is governed by the norms established by the diocesan bishop.

—Code of Canon Law (CCL), 536.1–2

committee, social concerns and education committees, and members from the parish at large;

- consist of members that reflect the diversity of the parish, representing different age groups, social classes and geographical areas, and persons who reflect the wisdom of the parish community as a whole;

- be composed of a chairperson and a vice-chairperson, secretary, and pastor or parish administrator who can form an "executive committee," that may assist in setting the agenda and conduct emergency parish business;

- conduct monthly meetings in a spirit of prayer and maintain confidentiality on matters so designated;

- promote evangelization and outreach to others, including ecumenical and inter-faith activity; uphold the teaching of the Catholic faith to all generations; encourage a Christian spirit through social justice action; and further the corporal and spiritual works of mercy with a vision of Christian stewardship of finances, personnel, and action.

The Parish Liturgy Committee

From the above list, it is clear that liturgy should be included on the pastoral council's agenda. In fact, committees for liturgy, education (catechesis), and social justice (action) are the three committees that usually flow from or are a subset of the parish pastoral council; however, other committees may be established in the community as well.[3] In many places a member of each of these committees serves as a representative to the pastoral council on behalf of the work of the committee they serve. The pastoral council and its committees are called to listen to the Christian faithful who "are free to make known their needs, . . . especially spiritual ones, and their desires."[4]

The liturgy committee does more than prepare and evaluate the liturgies in the parish. The committee prays well together and assists the community in its public prayer. It sets goals, direction, and principles for the liturgical life of the community. The committee functions as a sounding board for the parishioners and is comfortable with asking and taking on challenging questions and issues. The committee works hard at celebrating well—providing a basis for what they need and valuing the liturgy as the most important work of the parish community.

A brief job description of a parish liturgy committee includes the following:

- pays primary attention on doing the basics especially well, Sunday after Sunday—the essential actions of gathering, welcoming, proclaiming and reflecting on the word of God, and celebrating Eucharist;

- assesses and evaluates the needs of the worshipping assembly;

- advises and provides direction for those who prepare liturgies, including the parish liturgist, musicians, and presiding ministers;

- offers liturgical catechesis, for the liturgy and from the liturgy, to all parishioners;

- promotes the development of competent liturgical ministers and works to create guidelines and patterns for all liturgical ministers; sacramental, devotional and domestic Church celebrations; weekday Masses; special feasts; and holy days of obligation;

- sets goals for the progress of the liturgical, sacramental, and devotional life of the parish;

- implements directives from the universal Church, the diocesan Church, and the local parish;

- maintains ongoing communication with the pastoral council, other parish committees, and organizations.

Who Serves on a Parish Liturgy Committee?

The pastoral council and the liturgy committee should have a close relationship. It works well if a member of the parish liturgy committee serves on the pastoral council as a way of opening and maintaining the channels of communication. Both the pastoral council and liturgy committee are reflections of the community which it leads and serves. Just as the diocesan liturgical committee advises and serves the Bishop and the members of the local church,[5] so too does the liturgy committee serve as a resource for the local parish faith community. Feel free to contact your diocesan Office for Divine Worship to see if it offers training sessions for the parish or provides samples of some of the documentation you will need, such as sample meeting agendas/formats, job descriptions, prayers, and evaluation forms.

If you are building a committee from the ground up, the pastor or pastoral administrator may wish to appoint parish members based on experience, qualifications, and skills as collaborative leaders. If you already have a committee in place, consider a process of nomination or application, review, and election, or a process of discernment when seeking new members for the committee. Each parishioner who is seeking membership on the committee should be provided with a written job description that includes the number of monthly hours that the members would need to be available for service to the liturgy and the parish.

The members of the committee, therefore, should be an eclectic representation of the parish, be registered parishioners, and model full, conscious, and active participation in the liturgical and sacramental life of the community. Since the cooperation and leadership of the presiding minister is essential to any good liturgical celebration, the pastor and others who preside should play an active role in this committee. In addition, the committee should include the parish liturgist, music director (or a representative from the various music groups in the parish), and a representative from each of the liturgical ministries (lectors, servers, ushers/greeters, etc.). Rounding out membership on the committee includes the director of parish faith formation, the director of Christian initiation (or a member of the catechumenal team), along with several at-large members (including youth!).[6]

Qualities of a Committee Member

The qualifications of those who might serve on the committee include

- those with a knowledge of (or those who seek to know more about) liturgy and ritual;

- those comfortable with the principles of both preparing and evaluating the liturgy;

- those who embrace the teachings of the Church and the mandates of the Second Vatican Council;

- those who are generous with their time and talent, are charitable and conscious of the needs of the assembly, and those who love beauty.

When new members join the committee, be sure to pray for and bless their service. Below is a prayer you might use from the *Book of Blessings*, 1927.

Almighty God,
we give you thanks
for the many and varied ways you build up your Church.

Bless these officers of the [liturgy committee].
Grant that through their vision and direction
they may be of service to this parish
and bring honor and glory to your name.
Grant this through Christ our Lord.

Amen.

Electing a Chairperson, Vice-Chairperson, and Secretary

Members of the liturgy committee may select designated leaders (chairperson and vice-chairperson) as well as a person to record the minutes of the meeting (secretary). These individuals, along with the pastor and/or pastoral administrator, serve as the "executive committee." A discernment process should take place at a meeting early in the year to decide who the chairperson and secretary for the committee will be.[7] This service could be for three years and may be renewed for an additional three years. However, it is important for others to step up to the plate and assume leadership as well. Rotating one or two new people into the committee each year will be important for keeping the focus of the group fresh and alive with new insights and observations.

The number of people serving on the committee will vary from place to place. In a small or rural parish it may be three to four members. In larger parishes, generally eight to ten members is a good number. A committee of more than twelve generally results in less productivity.

Of course, just as the liturgy committee is a subset of the pastoral council, the liturgy committee could have its own subcommittees for liturgical music, environment, and ritual and sacraments. These smaller working committees can prepare their work and have a representative report to the liturgy committee on their behalf.

The Liturgy Committee Meeting

Provided on page 89 is a sample agenda for a typical liturgy committee meeting. The agenda at each meeting should include the following: opening prayer, short catechesis, brief review of previous meeting (minutes), review of the current agenda, and brief follow up to pending or unresolved issues, as well as key issues surrounding the approaching season. A section of the meeting should always be dedicated to discussing the parish's celebration of Sunday Eucharist.

A meeting may also include an evaluation of a previous season and reports from those representing the various liturgical ministries. Over the course of a year, the committee may wish to explore topics such as liturgy basics, the liturgical year, liturgical spirituality, environment and art, music, budgets, salaries and job descriptions, liturgical ministers, catechesis for and from the liturgy, scripture proclamation and reflection, parish celebrations of the Order of Christian Funerals and sacramental rites, other liturgical rites including Sunday Celebrations in the Absence of a Priest, blessings from the *Book of Blessings*, and the Liturgy of the Hours.

Additional topics for study and discussion might include building and/or renovation of the worship space, full inclusion of youth/children in the liturgy, liturgical training, mentoring younger Catholics, renewing returning Catholics, and providing new Catholics with liturgical catechesis and preparation. All meetings should conclude with a closing prayer.

Prayer during Meetings

Communal prayer plays an important role in the meeting of the liturgy committee. We know that Jesus said that "where two or three are gathered in my name, there am I in the midst of them,"[8] and we are aware of the Lord's command to "pray without ceasing."[9] Consider building the prayer around the seasonal psalm,[10] the psalm of the Sunday or the day, and/or a section of one of the prefaces for the following Sunday or season. The prayer might also include a short scripture passage, intercessory prayer, and the Lord's Prayer. You might consider beginning your meetings with the prayer that was used before every session of the Second Vatican Council.

*We stand before you, Holy Spirit
conscious of our sinfulness,
but aware that we gather in your name.*

*Come to us, remain with us,
and enlighten our hearts.*

*Give us light and strength
to know your will,
to make it our own,
and to live it in our lives.*

*Guide us by your wisdom,
support us by your power,
for you are God,
sharing the glory of Father and Son.*

*You desire justice for all:
enable us to uphold the rights of others;
do not allow us to be mislead by ignorance
or corrupted by fear or favor.*

*Unite us to yourself in the bond of love
and keep us faithful to all that is true.*

*As we gather in your name
may we temper justice with love,
so that all our decisions
may be pleasing to you,
and earn the reward
promised to good and faithful servants.
You live and reign with the Father and the Son,
one God, for ever and ever.
Amen.*

Different members of the committee can take turns leading the prayer each time the committee meets, but strive for a consistent pattern. Since the liturgy itself follows a structure, try to model the prayer at the meeting using a common pattern or structure. For example, if your committee usually prays by beginning with the Sign of the Cross, the recitation of a psalm, a reading from scripture, and concludes with a closing prayer, continue this practice at each meeting.

A Mission Statement

It is important for a parish liturgy committee to prepare a mission statement and visit it at each meeting. To do this, start by looking at the committee's mission statement for both the parish and the pastoral council. The mission statement should flow from these two statements. Mission statements are usually composed of four major areas. These areas can provide a helpful framework for guiding the work of your commission, including the following:

1. **Identity.** Points to the identifying elements of the parish (name, location, distinctive character, and history). For example: *We, the members of the liturgical committee of the faith community of N . . . .*

2. **Purpose.** Focuses on the core values, beliefs, and the reason for the committee. For example: *. . . committed to the full, conscious, and active participation of all in the liturgy, we value . . . .*

3. **Function.** Identifies the commitments of the committee, what the committee does in general, and to whom it is directed. For example: *We are committed to . . . .*

4. **Future.** Addresses areas of challenge and elements that need strengthening. For example: *We seek to become . . . .*

Here is a sample mission statement:

The members of the liturgy committee of Saint N. _____, guided by the Trinity of three persons in one God, Father, Son, and Holy Spirit, commit ourselves to joyfully working together and promoting the full, conscious, and active participation of all who seek to worship the God of spirit and truth through our faith community's liturgies. We strive to prepare liturgical and sacramental celebrations that model the Church as the sacrament of unity, build up the body of Christ, reflect the diversity of our faith community, and embrace with love and welcome the most vulnerable in our midst.

Regularly address the mission statement at meetings to make sure that its objective is clear and is being fulfilled. The statement could be included as part of the prayer each time the committees meets. Here is a sample prayer that incorporates pieces of the parish mission statement for use during the meeting of the liturgy committee:

> *God of all grace,*
> *we come before you to commit ourselves*
> *to joyfully working together and promoting*
> *the full, conscious, and active participation*
> *of all who seek to worship you through our faith*
> *community's liturgies.*
> *Help us to prepare liturgical and sacramental celebrations*
> *that model the Church as the sacrament of unity,*
> *that build up the body of Christ,*
> *that reflect the diversity of our faith community,*
> *and that embrace with love and welcome*
> *the most vulnerable in our midst.*
> *We call on the intercession of our parish patron*
> *Saint N._____*
> *and ask that you guide our preparation and evaluation.*
> *We ask this through Christ our Lord.*
> *Amen.*

The Liturgy Committee and the Faith Formation Team

The liturgy committee will need to have a good working relationship with the religious education/faith formation catechists and their director(s). These folks who coordinate infant Baptism, first Penance, first Holy Communion, Confirmation, and perhaps even the Rite of Christian Initiation of Adults' formation team should be in constant dialogue with the parish liturgy committee. The liturgy committee should work with the religious education staff to establish sacramental preparation guidelines and patterns for the way in which the sacraments are celebrated in the community.

FORMULATION OF LITURGICAL GUIDELINES FOR OTHER RITES: It is important to have clear liturgical guidelines that respect the rites and are at the same time pastoral and flexible. The Church never denies the celebration of the sacraments to anyone free of impediments; she may delay the celebration, but no one is to be denied access to the sacraments. When guidelines are in place, the parish can provide the appropriate tools for those who are preparing for the sacraments and those who may need to have the celebration of the sacraments delayed. Formulation of liturgical guidelines for the parish celebration of the sacraments—especially regarding funerals, weddings, infant Baptism, and Christian initiation for children, youth, and adults—are the first to formulate if no guidelines are yet in place.

Don't feel like you have to reinvent the wheel. Call your diocesan Office for Worship and ask for some sample guidelines or check with a neighboring parish to see what is in place there. It is also recommended to craft guidelines that are similar in scope for all the parishes in the same city or area. This will be a valuable source of catechesis for people who tend to shop around and inquire about celebrating the sacraments, often on their terms, especially infant Baptism, Marriage, Rite of Christian Initiation of Adults, and funeral liturgies. The diocese usually has guidelines and policies that will support what you put into place. Remember the principle of charity, especially at the time of a person's death. If the family and friends of the deceased have a good experience with the Church and her ministers, they may return to the parish rather than when the experience may not be so positive and find that they may choose not to return to the house of the Church.

Concern for the Details

There is often a tension between the "nuts and bolts" of preparing particular liturgies and providing liturgical formation. For example, does the liturgy committee simply decide who's going to buy flowers—and what kind of flowers—or does the committee deal with deeper concepts and issues? Here we follow a simple principle—*leave these and other decisions to the "experts."* Who are the experts? They will be different folks in every community. They could be paid or volunteer, full time or part time, and they could serve as pastoral associate, director of liturgy, director of liturgy and music, or just director of music. The experts can also be a group of talented individuals who form subcommittees of the liturgy committee to prepare the music, the environment, and the various rites.

Because liturgy is at the heart of parish life, the liturgy committee and its work need to be among the highest priorities. The parish liturgy committee should understand that its primary responsibility is not necessarily to prepare the details for liturgical celebrations. The committee's primary role is *setting a vision* for the celebration of the liturgy in the community and providing liturgical formation for its members and the entire parish. Since liturgy is a work of art, it should be prepared by artists. Whether it is a small group of experts or members of the parish liturgy committee who are charged with the task of preparing and evaluating the liturgy, everyone involved in the process must know, love, and respect the members of the liturgical assembly.

Conflict Resolution

Sometimes during meetings there can be tension between the parish professional (pastor, trained liturgist, professional music director) and the untrained, good-hearted volunteer. One must always remember to work out of the principle of charity. While conflict or tensions may occasionally rise to the surface in a meeting, all need to reverence the dignity of the human person and strive for a charitable outcome and resolution. In *extreme* cases—if conflict is unresolved—it may be necessary to bring in a facilitator to work with the group. The final decision in the parish always lies with the pastor or pastoral administrator. Committee members, pastoral administrators, pastors, and other staff members should always strive to support and facilitate a collaborative model for building up the body of Christ.

The Liturgy Committee and the Parish

Parish Involvement

It is extremely important that members of the liturgy committee are involved in the parish—being present and actively participating at liturgies. If the parish has more than one liturgy on a weekend, members of the committee should occasionally participate in the various services. Committee members should participate in the annual celebration of the Paschal Triduum and occasionally attend sacramental rites, parish devotions, funerals, and other prayer services. Only in this way can members of the liturgy committee have a true and authentic understanding and experience of the worship life of their parish community.

Communication with other Committees

The liturgy committee will want to be in regular dialogue with other parish committees, especially the pastoral council. Dialogue is essential to keep lines of communication open so the pastoral council and parish staff members will not be faced with any surprises, and that they can have an opportunity for dialogue and collaboration with any changes that may be implemented into the liturgical life of the parish. If the parish has an altar society or guild, it would be important to collaborate with these folks, and perhaps even have one of them serve on the liturgy committee. In many parishes the members of these societies and guilds often raise funds for liturgical appointments and materials.

It is important that members of the liturgy committee be involved with the parish—being present and actively participating at liturgies.

Liturgy Committee and the Assembly

The parish liturgy committee and its members are ambassadors to the assembly—as a group and as individuals—listening for questions and concerns and relaying them to other members of the committee, communicating, and building interest and enthusiasm about the liturgy. Therefore, the liturgy committee must know, love, and respect the assembly. Establishing relationships with all in the assembly will serve the committee well. Knowing the ages, races, ethnicities, languages, cultures, socioeconomic statuses, and education levels of the parishioners will be of great benefit to the committee and the parish. Gleaning this knowledge is critical if the committee hopes to be in touch with the worshipping community's hopes, dreams, fears, and struggles or to understand and support the way in which the community prays, gestures, sings, and listens during liturgical celebrations.

Members of the liturgy committee should know, love, and respect their faith community.

The Liturgy Committee and Ongoing Formation

Attending Liturgy at Other Churches

It is desirable that members of the committee attend liturgies outside of the parish. A good place to start is at the other parishes in the same deanery or vicariate. A visit to the diocesan cathedral at least once a year is a must for all members of the liturgy committee. The cathedral, as the mother church, is "a model for the other churches of the diocese in its conformity to the directives laid down in the liturgical documents and books."[11] In addition, attendance at the Chrism Mass, Rite of Election, ordination, or another diocesan celebration at the cathedral can be a beneficial experience for members of the parish liturgy committee. By attending a diocesan celebration at the cathedral, members of the parish can experience liturgy celebrated in its fullest expression: a representative number of the faithful gathered around the Lord's table under the leadership of the local Bishop and his priests.

Liturgical Workshops, Conferences, and Schools

In order to provide members of the parish liturgy committee with continuing formation and education about the liturgy, encourage

When visiting other parishes, return with the parish bulletin or any other publications that will benefit your community. Bring a camera. Taking pictures of various worship spaces and decor will be helpful to the work of the committee.

your folks to attend liturgical conferences and workshops. It is most desirable to attend these workshops and conferences together as a committee or as individuals. Every member of the liturgy committee should have a basic understanding of the following: the scope and sequence of the liturgical year; the basic structure of the Order of Mass; a basic understanding of how to use the Lectionary, Sacramentary (Roman Missal) and Ordo; a working knowledge of the liturgical documents, and a familiarity with the various sacramental rites of the Church, especially the Rite of Christian Initiation of Adults.

In many places, the diocesan Office for Divine Worship offers various workshops and training programs/sessions for liturgical ministers throughout the year. Many liturgical and music publishers, groups, and organizations offer workshops, conferences, and seminars. Here is a list of a few organizations that provide excellent formation programs:

1. The National Association of Pastoral Musicians
   conventions, schools, and study days
   www.npm.org

2. The Federation of Diocesan Liturgical Committees
   workshops and study days
   www.fdlc.org

3. The Southwest Liturgical Conference
   workshops and study days
   www.swlc.org

4. The North American Forum on the Catechumenate
   institutes and workshops
   www.naforum.org

5. National Pastoral Life Center
   conferences, institutes, and lectures
   www.nplc.org

The major Catholic music publishers (GIA, OCP, and WLP) offer workshops, seminars, and formation days for pastoral musicians and liturgists.[12] The following universities offer programs, classes, institutes, and conferences:

1. Saint John's University (MN)
   School of Theology • Seminary
   www.csbsju.edu/sot

2. The University of Dayton (OH)
   Institute for Liturgical Ministry
   www.ilmdayton.org

3. The University of Notre Dame (IN)
   Department of Theology
   theology.nd.edu

4. University of Santa Clara (CA)
   Graduate program in pastoral ministry
   www.scu.edu/ecppm/pastoralministries

5. University of St. Mary of the Lake/Mundelein Seminary (IL)
   Liturgical Institute
   www.usml.edu/liturgicalinstitute/liturgicalinstitute.htm

Ten Tenets for Liturgy Committees

We conclude this chapter with ten tenets that the members of the parish liturgy committee should hold in their minds and hearts. Come back to these tenets throughout the year. They will be very useful as a guide for discussion and evaluation of your parish liturgies.

1. Scripture is at the heart of all liturgy.

2. Baptism, as the door to all the sacraments, invites us into community and the Church's worship.

3. Sunday, the Lord's Day, is the primary time for the whole community to worship the Trinity—God the Father, Son, and Holy Spirit.

4. Liturgy is the source and summit of Christian worship, prayer, and service.

5. Liturgy always celebrates and embraces the Paschal Mystery, which includes the Incarnation, life, death, Resurrection, Ascension, and Pentecost events.

6. Know and study the resources: ritual books and their introductions, the documents of the Second Vatican Council, the Code of Canon Law, along with documents from the Vatican and your Conference of Bishops.

7. Liturgy is marked by noble simplicity and honesty.

8. Progressive solemnity guides us in preparation and celebration of the liturgy. When we prepare the liturgy, we choose only those elements appropriate to the Sunday or season. For example, the Sundays of Easter would be celebrated with greater solemnity than those of Ordinary Time.

9. Liturgy is inheritably musical, and our focus should be singing the liturgy, not singing at the liturgy. So our first choice is the ritual dialogues, followed by the acclamations and other texts of the liturgy rather than singing just hymns or songs at the liturgy.

10. The aim to be considered before all else, as we are reminded in CSL, 14, is the full, conscious, and active participation of all the faithful in the worship of the Trinity.[13]

The Body of Christ, the "chosen race, a royal priesthood, a holy nation, a redeemed people" (1 Peter 2:9; see 2:4–5),"[14] is composed of many limbs attached to the Head, Christ our Lord. Each member of the Body is called to enter into the liturgy fully, consciously, and actively.[15] An active parish liturgy committee can assist in implementing the mandates of the Second Vatican Council and make this participation a reality in each parish. We hope this book has provided you with a bursting tool belt full of ways to enter into the mystery of faith.

Questions for Discussion and Reflection

1. What are the principal elements to consider when preparing the Sunday Mass? How are these principles applied to each liturgical season and each celebration of the sacraments?

_____

_____

_____

2. What are the principal elements to consider when evaluating the Sunday Mass? How are these principles applied to each liturgical season and each celebration of the sacraments?

_____

_____

_____

3. If "full, conscious, and active participation is the aim to be considered before all else,"[16] in the celebration of the liturgy, what are some concrete ways in which you can achieve this goal in your parish?

_____

_____

_____

4. Given the makeup of your parish, how many people should serve on your parish liturgy committee? Who might these people be? What will be their job description, and how will they interface with the parish pastoral council, the pastor, pastoral administrator, the community?

_____

_____

_____

NOTES

1. As a consultative body, the pastoral council advises, but the final decision rests with the pastor and/or pastoral administrator or other designated staff member.

2. See *Code of Canon Law*, §536.

3. See The *Code of Canon Law: A Text and Commentary* states: "The forum provided by the council enables all to collaborate in fostering pastoral activity, i.e., an organized, unified endeavor, which broadly includes liturgy, education, social service, evangelization, mission activity, family life, communications, ecumenism, and administration. Parish council committees frequently correspond to these areas of concern" (p. 432). Coriden, James A., Thomas J. Green, Donald E. Huntschel, eds. *Code of Canon Law: A Text and Commentary* (Mahweh, NJ: Paulist Press, 1985).

4. Canon 212 §2.

5. See CSL, 45.

6. Often the liturgy committee will formulate various subcommittees to take care of "nuts and bolts" details. Such subcommittees include liturgical environment and art and liturgical music. Representatives from these subcommittees should also attend the primary meetings of the liturgy committee.

7. See Appendix III on page 97.

8. Matthew 18:20.

9. 1 Thessalonians 5:17; see also Luke 18:1.

10. The seasonal psalms can be found in the Lectionary, #174.

11. *Ceremonial of Bishops*, 46.

12. Refer to page 79 in the Resources section for contact information.

13. Adapted from Belford, William, Glenn C. J. Byer, and Michael R. Prendergast. *Parish Liturgy Basics* (Portland, OR: Pastoral Press, 2005).

14. CSL, 14.

15. See CSL, 14.

16. CSL, 14 (Vatican translation).

Frequently Asked Questions

The questions that liturgy committee members regularly deal with are vast and range from the complex to the simple, from general to specific. What follows are common questions that most committees will encounter.

General Questions

1. *What is the difference between a liturgy committee and a liturgy preparation team?*

Many liturgy committees get bogged down trying to do detailed preparation for the weekly celebration of the liturgy instead of dealing with the larger issues. Normally a liturgy committee deals with broad, over-reaching issues and leaves the details of liturgy preparation to the experts (the pastor, pastoral associate, music director, and/or liturgist) or a small band of faithful workers and collaborators. For example, a liturgy committee can deal with larger questions about the state of liturgical music in the parish, and a preparation team or individual expert can surface specific repertoire ideas. In most cases, the actual choice of music should be left to the music director. Just as a preacher may seek out input in preparing a homily,[1] these collaborators may provide input to the homilist but obviously they do not actually write the homily.

2. *How can we better educate members of our liturgy committees in the theology of Eucharist and practices within the local church so that they can continue the liturgical renewal of assemblies? Is that an appropriate task for the liturgy committee?*

Catechesis, catechesis, catechesis has been the rallying cry of many since the Second Vatican Council. So often we have missed opportunities for catechesis. The *Constitution on the Sacred Liturgy* reminds us of the importance of "liturgical instruction of the faithful and their active participation, internal and external, in the liturgy, taking into account their age, condition, way of life and standard of religious culture."[2] The parish liturgy committee should study the principles of liturgy and ritual as found in the basic documents[3] so they can assist in the formation of their sisters and brothers in the faith community. The *Mystery of Faith*, published by the Federation of Diocesan Liturgical Commissions, is an excellent resource to use in forming committees about the structure and history of the Order of Mass and then sharing that information with the wider community.

3. I want to start a liturgy committee in my parish. Where do I begin?

The Second Vatican Council saw the value of having a group of experts in the field of liturgy, sacred music, and sacred art consult with each diocesan Bishop.[4] Likewise, a parish liturgy committee can be of great service to the pastor or the pastoral administrator of a parish. Select members who love the Church and her liturgy, those who participate fully in the liturgical life of the parish along with a representative from the various liturgical ministries in the parish (e.g. musicians, extraordinary ministers of Holy Communion, lectors, artists, and of course the pastor and or other clergy on the staff). The committee should begin by seeking liturgical formation and study of the Church's teaching of liturgy, ritual, music, and art. Studying the Church's documents on the liturgy, and reading books related to liturgical topics and articles found in liturgical journals is a good place to start. You may also wish to consult with your diocesan office of worship to see what support they will provide for you. A component of each meeting should always include some formation. Members should reflect the population of the entire parish, including age, gender, racial and ethnic considerations, etc. A liturgical committee is generally responsible for the following:

1. oversight of the faith community's worship;

2. formation and training of liturgical ministers;

3. ongoing catechesis and formation of the worshipping assembly;

4. oversight of parish patterns and policies concerning the worshipping community;

5. reviews and implements directives coming from the local Bishop or his representative;

6. members always strive to work out of a principle of charity and put aside personal likes and dislikes so the aim of the worshipping community and its liturgies are always seen as "the sacrament of unity";[5]

7. seasonally evaluates the liturgical celebrations of the worshipping community.

Advertise! Parishes often benefit by publishing a pamphlet/booklet outlining all the ministries, committees, and organizations in the parish. This includes a brief description of the ministry, the name of the coordinator, and necessary contact information. These booklets can be available in the vestibule, parish center, or parish office. This same information should also be accessible on the parish Web site.

Consider advertising in the parish bulletin and on the web site. Annual ministry fairs are also a good way to personally invite interested parishioners to join committees and serve as liturgical ministers.

4. *Sometimes our committee has prepared something and it gets changed at the last minute by someone on the staff or in one of the other ministries. It's very frustrating! What can we do to prevent this?*

It's very important to coordinate with the other liturgical ministers and staff. Be sure a representative of your team attends the meetings of the parish liturgy committee or consults regularly with someone from the staff and the other liturgical ministries. Over time you will come to know the concerns of the other participants in liturgy preparation, but it's always smart and considerate to communicate frequently with everyone concerned. Charity is paramount in any ministry and keeps us focused on our ultimate goals.[6]

5. *How does the parish liturgy committee deal with change and progress or resistance from parishioners when implementing approved liturgical changes? What is the process for change, and how fast do you make the change?*

Here we will state emphatically about the importance of catechesis. A one-time bulletin announcement or flyer or even a one-time announcement as part of the homily at Mass will not do. We do a disservice to the worshipping community when we do not provide adequate and ongoing liturgical catechesis. Provide ongoing adult faith formation sessions.

Study the liturgy in religious education classes. Invite speakers to instruct the committee members.

Liturgical Preparation Questions

The following are common and very specific questions that often come up at liturgy committee meetings concerning liturgical preparation.

1. *Our committee has been discussing implementing the Liturgy of the Hours. What are some things we should consider?*

Throughout the ages, the Church has remained faithful to "pray always," as Jesus instructed in Luke 18:1 and Paul told the Thessalonians.[7] Part of the Church's tradition in carrying out this teaching has been the celebration of the Liturgy of the Hours. Here are some things to consider when implementing the Liturgy of the Hours in the parish.

The celebration of Morning and Evening Prayer is an important element in the liturgical life of each parish community. The celebration of the Liturgy of the Hours in the parish church must be seen as an ecclesial liturgy with both clergy and laity celebrating together as a community of prayer. The Liturgy of the Hours in any parish community is an exercise of baptismal ministry. When celebrating the Hours, the parish community enters into the rhythm of the liturgical year and experiences more fully the Paschal Mystery.

The most common practice for celebrating the Liturgy of the Hours in parish communities today seems to be during the major seasons. Many communities gather for the celebration of Sunday Evening Prayer during the Advent and Christmas seasons or the Lent/Triduum/Easter seasons. In addition, many communities, especially those without resident priests, gather to celebrate Morning or Evening Prayer.

Pastoral practice must take into consideration the human needs of modern Christians. When we attempt to restore the Liturgy of the Hours, we must adapt to the demands placed upon the fabric of the human family.

Celebrations of the Hours that are lengthy and fail to engage the hearts of the faithful through symbol, gesture, ritual, and song may hinder the process. The celebration of the Hours can provide a healing rhythm for people caught in the frenzied pace of twenty-first century living. The music and liturgical symbols of light and incense can carry us beyond the present into the Paschal Mystery.

If Morning and Evening Prayer are to be introduced to the community, it should follow the basic structure of the Office and include hymnody, psalmody, a reading, canticle, intercessions, and the Lord's Prayer. Other elements can be included such as the prayer of thanksgiving and the Service of Light. The ritual action (prayer and ceremonial), the symbols of light, incense, and water as well as posture, gesture, movement, and silence are all used and focused on the primary symbol—that of the gathered assembly. The prayer, posture, gesture, movement, and silence all become the living action of the assembly. It is important that the first taste of Morning and Evening Prayer be a good experience. Careful preparation and celebration of these liturgies is essential. The communal celebration of the Liturgy of the Hours can take a community beyond itself and aid in the realization that God is in the world among them as flesh and blood. At the Liturgy of the Hours, we are celebrating the reign of God—the tension between our lives and God's will for humanity.

Many musical resources abound for implementing the celebration of the Hours. These include "Praise God in Song" (various), "Light and Peace" (Haas), and "Holden Evening Prayer" (Haugen);[8] "Lord, Open My Lips" (Consiglio) and "O Joyful Light" (Joncas);[9] "God of Light be Praised" (various) and "Jesus When the Sun Goes Down" (Janco);[10] "Pray Without Ceasing" (various);[11] and the "Mundelein Psalter" (Martis).[12]

In addition to the official four-volume set of the *Liturgy of the Hours* or the one-volume *Christian Prayer*, both available from Catholic Book Publishing, the following belong in parish libraries: *An Everyday Book of Hours* and *A Seasonal Book of Hours*, both by William G. Storey and available from LTP. LTP has additional resources for praying the hours of the day and the seasons.

Start small. Begin parish meetings and formation sessions, scripture groups, and other activities with the Hours. And not just with adults—with children and teens! Remember the cliché, "if you build it they will come." Before you know it, a small prayer group can become a celebration of the greater parish community.[13]

2. *After evaluating our parish liturgies, our committee determined that it is too rushed and has no time for communal and personal reflection. How might silence be integrated into the liturgy? Where is silence appropriate?*

A primary theme of liturgical reform in the *Constitution on the Sacred Liturgy*, the liturgy constitution of the Second Vatican Council, is *active participation*. It is the "aim to be considered before all else."[14] But active participation is not activism, as if we must get the assembly to do something. Participation is entering into the heart of the mystery celebrated in the liturgy. Just as acclamations, responses, gestures, hymns, and posture are means of participation, so is silence: At the proper times all should observe a reverent silence.[15] Neither an exception to, nor contrast to participation, silence is a profound manner of active participation. The *General Instruction of the Roman Missal* recommends that silence be incorporated into the liturgy at the following moments: "within the Act of Penitence and again after the invitation to pray . . . at the conclusion of a reading or the homily . . . [and] after Communion. . . ."[16] In addition to during the liturgy, the General Instruction recommends that "even before the celebration itself, it is commendable that silence . . . be observed in the church, in the sacristy, in the vesting room, and in adjacent areas. . . ."[17]

Here are some things for members of the liturgy committee to reflect upon and consider.

FOR THOSE WHO PREPARE THE LITURGY:

- Through adult education classes or articles in a bulletin or newsletter, educate the assembly about the role of silence.

- Educate liturgical ministers about the role of silence in their annual training and enrichment sessions.

- Develop criteria with the priest and the other liturgical ministers, so that all have a common understanding of when silence will be kept, how long it will kept, and who will set the pace. For example, develop a policy about whether the silence after the Second Reading is timed by the celebrant (who stands for the Gospel) or by the musicians (who begin the Gospel Acclamation).

- Offer reminders to the liturgical ministers, for example, in their instruction sheets, or in notes on their music.

- Move slowly in increasing the amount of silence, with feedback on how it is being experienced. Take care to explain what is being done and listen to the reactions.

- Periodically remind yourself and others about the practice of keeping silence, so that the silence does not gradually get shortened or lost over time.

FOR ALL LITURGICAL MINISTERS:

- It may sound obvious, and yet we all need to be reminded: pray during the liturgy! Learn to treasure the silence as a time of entering more deeply into the liturgy.

- Prepare yourself *before* the liturgy, so that practical concerns (location of music, determination of reading option to be proclaimed, setting of ribbons) do not take over silent time during the liturgy.

- Eliminate pauses resulting from planning difficulties. Pauses *after* something (e.g., a reading, a chant, Communion, the invitation "Let us pray") have a purpose. Pauses *before* something are sometimes experienced as an uneasy delay. An example: a long pause while the first reader walks up to the ambo is a delay. Instruct readers to be ready to begin the reading as soon as all are seated and settled.

- Renew the discipline of daily silent prayer outside the liturgy.

- Use liturgical silence to offer your ministry to God. A way of dealing with nervousness is to pray silently: "It is all right. I am letting go of myself and trusting God. I am accepted by God and this community, and so is my ministry. I am at peace."

FOR CATECHISTS AND TEACHERS:

- Teach about the role of silence in the liturgy in age-appropriate ways.

- Use silent prayer during classes and meeting sessions. For example, model liturgical prayer in the classroom by using the invitation "Let us pray" followed by silent time, before offering a spoken prayer.

FOR PRIEST CELEBRANTS:

- Say what you mean and mean what the liturgy says. If you mean, "Let us stand for the Prayer after Communion," then do not say, "Let us pray." Gesture for all to stand, and when all are standing, say, "Let us pray."

- Discipline yourself to maintain silence after the invitation, "Let us pray." If necessary, count slowly to 20, so that the pauses do not get lost.

- Make sure that the pauses are reflective prayer and not a time to get organized, e.g., gesturing to a server or finding a prayer in the Roman Missal.

- Develop a sense of the assembly's comfort level with silence. Be sensitive to signs of restlessness. Ask for feedback.

- To focus your homily, think of the silent time after the homily as the goal of preaching. At daily Mass, for example, where the homily is generally brief, considering the homily as an introduction to the silence that will follow can help ensure that you have only one main point, a point that moves the listener to prayerful reflection.[18]

3. *My parish is evolving as a multi-cultural community. Where should we begin the discussion or implementation of liturgical inculturation?*

Almost every faith community in the United States and Canada contains people of various cultures and language speaking groups. Inculturation is a growing reality in the North American Church and one that deserves (and needs) careful attention and consideration. There are no simple answers, and it goes well beyond offering a Mass in Polish, reciting the Rosary in Vietnamese, or singing a Spanish song every once in a while. Members of the parish liturgy committee (indeed, the entire parish) must establish relationships with parishioners from other cultures. By doing so it will be easier to invite and entertain various cultural traditions into the liturgy.

Franciscan brother Rufino Zaragosa suggests that there are seven gestures of intercultural hospitality and sensitivity:[19]

1. Eat new foods.

2. Request a cultural mentor.

3. Make personal invitations.

4. Listen to songs and stories.

5. Identify resistance.

6. Inform the dominant culture.

7. Collaborate.

Inculturation is a growing reality in the North American Church and one that deserves (and needs!) careful attention and consideration.

These seven gestures are based on the principle that "no liturgy, however welcoming and participatory, can substitute for a truly multicultural approach to pastoral care in the parish at large. Extra-liturgical interaction and cooperation among the various groups in the parish serves as the indispensable context for multicultural liturgy."[20] If communities are attentive to these steps they will find people of "every race, language and way of life"[21] in our faith communities and soon discover that their traditions, languages, and ways of life can only enhance our experience of praise and worship of our God. In this way, we become truly one body in Christ. For resources concerning inculturation, please refer to the Resources section on page 72.

4. *In my parish, the extraordinary ministers of Holy Communion often have to go to the tabernacle to retrieve reserved hosts because they run out during the distribution of Holy Communion. The liturgy committee has been charged with the task of alleviating this problem. What can be done to ensure that the correct number of hosts is consecrated during Mass so that the ministers do not need to use the reserved hosts?*

In the celebration of Eucharist the gifts of bread and wine are brought to the table by members of the assembly during the Preparation of the Gifts and the Altar.[22] This is a clear sign that the symbols of bread and wine are the food and drink for this sacred meal. At Eucharist, the preferred principle is that all the bread and wine used at a given Mass should be consecrated at that Mass.[23] The distribution of already consecrated hosts from the tabernacle should clearly be an exception rather than the norm.

The encyclicals of Pope Benedict XIV *Certiores Effecti* (1742) and *Mediator Dei* of Pope Pius XII (1947) containing statements emphasizing the importance of the assembly receiving bread consecrated at the same Mass, suggest that this is a constant teaching of the Church.[24] The liturgical documents from the Second Vatican Council affirm these teachings:

> That more perfect form of participation in the Mass whereby the faithful, after the priest's communion, receive the Lord's Body from the same sacrifice, is warmingly recommended.[25]

> It is most desirable that the faithful, just as the priest himself is bound to do, receive the Lord's body from hosts consecrated at the same Mass and that, in the instances when it is permitted, they partake of the chalice . . . so that even by means of the signs Communion will stand out more clearly as a participation in the sacrifice actually being celebrated.[26]

If, at a parish celebration of Eucharist, the priest or the extraordinary ministers of Holy Communion foresee that they may run out of consecrated bread, they should first check with one another. If there are only a small number of communicants, they should begin to break the Eucharistic bread into smaller pieces to share with the faithful who have not yet received Holy Communion. Only after exhausting these two possibilities would they go to the tabernacle to bring the reserved hosts to be shared with the assembly.

Most parish communities, both large and small, can estimate rather closely the number of weekly communicants. In most situations, the size of a given assembly will not vary widely from week to week. Each faith community should train sacristans or other ministers to be attentive to preparing the amount of bread and wine used for each Eucharistic celebration.[27] The determination of the amount of bread and wine for the assembly should be one of the final functions of the sacristan or extraordinary ministers of Holy Communion prior to the beginning of Mass. However, they may have to make adjustments to the amount of bread and wine after the proclamation of the Gospel if necessary. The Church teaches that the reservation of Eucharist is to be reserved in parish churches primarily for the administration of *Viaticum* of the dying, secondly for giving Holy Communion to the sick outside of Mass, and finally for Eucharistic adoration.[28] There is no mention made in post-conciliar liturgical norms of reserving Eucharist for distribution at later Masses. Church documents insist on using bread and wine consecrated during that Mass for the reception of Holy Communion by the faithful.

The teaching of the Church is clear; enough bread and enough wine for each Eucharistic celebration. When we have a clear understanding about the role of the sacristan in preparing the right amount of bread and wine for each Mass, we can begin to eliminate the problem of consecrating too much Eucharistic bread for the celebration of Mass and thus always receive Holy Communion from the "sacrifice being celebrated" and not the tabernacle's supply.

5. Who should write the Prayer of the Faithful—is this the task of the liturgy committee? What are the guidelines for writing the petitions?

Several options are possible; one or two people from the liturgy committee, the deacon, and the pastor or liturgy director may prepare the Prayer of the Faithful. Remember, the intercessions are general in nature, not just specific (before the revised GIRM, they were referred to as just that—the General Intercessions). For example: *For Mary Smith and all who are suffering from illness, we pray,* versus, *For Mary Smith who is sick, we pray.*

Samples of intercession are found in Appendix I of the Roman Missal (Sacramentary) and printed by various publishers. All of these are meant to serve as models for the intercessions that are used in the parish each week.

A good rule of thumb for those who prepare the intercessions is to have the scripture of the day in one hand and any local newspaper in the other.

In general, the Prayer of the Faithful is offered first for the Church, then for public authorities and the salvation of the world, for those oppressed or burdened by various needs, and for the local community.[29]

6. *Members of our community would like to celebrate our parish feast day on a Sunday. Can we substitute the readings of our patron for the Sunday readings?*

Sunday, the Lord's Day is the day the Church celebrates the Paschal Mystery, and "other celebrations, unless they be truly of greatest importance, shall not have precedence over the Sunday, which is the foundation and kernel of the entire liturgical year."[30] The Table of Liturgical Days tells us that solemnities of the title of a particular church rank above feasts of the Lord in the General Calendar and above Sundays of the Christmas season and Sundays in Ordinary Time. So if you're a member of Saint Francis Church, you should celebrate the Memorial of Saint Francis as a solemnity and not the Twenty-seventh Sunday in Ordinary Time whenever October 4 lands on a Sunday. If your parish feast day is one that falls on a Sunday in Advent, Lent, or Easter, one may not substitute the readings or prayers from the observance of the parish's patron saint.

7. *How many readings must/should we do at the Easter Vigil?*

On this night the parish should try to take time to proclaim the seven readings from the Old Testament with their accompanying psalm and prayers and the two New Testament readings, namely from the apostle Paul and the Gospel. On this night the deeds of the history of salvation are recounted—beginning with Moses and all the prophets and ending with an explanation of the Paschal Mystery of Christ. *Paschale solemnitatis* ("On Preparing and Celebrating the Paschal Feasts") indicates that "all the readings should be read in order that the character of the Easter Vigil, which demands that it be somewhat prolonged, be respected at all costs."[31] The document continues by saying that when "pastoral conditions require that the number of readings be reduced, there should be at least three readings for the Old Testament—taken form the law and the prophets—and the reading from Exodus 14 with its canticle must never be omitted."[32] This instruction is repeated at #21 of the rubrics for the Paschal Vigil in the third edition of the Roman Missal. While we don't have an official translation as of yet, the Roman Missal says you reduce the readings for "*graviores*" pastoral conditions—that is, for rather serious ones—not just for any measly pastoral conditions. It also states that the respective psalms should be retained with each reading if the number of readings is reduced.

8. *When can the Easter Vigil service start? Why can't we have the regular Saturday vigil Mass instead of the long, drawn-out Easter Vigil service?*

The *General Norms for the Liturgical Year and Calendar,* (GNLYC, quoting Saint Augustine's sermon 219), refers to the Easter Vigil as "the mother of all vigils."[33] As such, the Church teaches that the "Easter Vigil should take place at night, that is, it should either begin after nightfall or end before the dawn of Sunday."[34] Even when Easter falls during daylight saving time the celebration should begin after dark (In 1987 the Bishops' Committee on the Liturgy suggested that dark would be about 90 minutes after sunset) so that when the celebration begins it *looks* like, *feels* like, and *is* night. At the same time, the fire might be lit at any time people would be turning on lights at home. You are more likely to get people to participate in the Vigil 30 minutes after nightfall rather than waiting for the full 90 minutes. The other option is the possibility of beginning the celebration in the early hours of the morning, coming to a conclusion just before dawn.[35]

9. *Where do you place the crèche at Christmas (and the Advent wreath during Advent)?*

The Advent wreath may be placed near the ambo or in the entrance to the church building somewhere visible to the assembly. One option would be to place the Advent wreath near the Marian shrine, for Mary is a model of waiting for the Lord. If your worship space allows, it may also be suspended from above either at the entrance to the prebyterium or over the assembly. Apart from the blessing on the First Sunday of Advent, there is no reference to the wreath in the liturgies of Advent. The wreath remains a special focus of prayer in the domestic church, the home.[36]

The crèche is best placed where people (including children) can interact with it on a human level. The order of blessing calls for the placement of the crèche in the church where it is easily accessible by the faithful but not in the (presbyteriun) sanctuary. The crèche should not be placed in front of the altar since it can reduce the altar to a simple backdrop instead of the central focus for the action of the celebration.[37]

> 10. *How many candles should be in the sanctuary, where are they placed, and may oil-burning candles be used?*

Candles, made of wax or of oil, are used in the celebration of Mass and other rites as a sign of reverence and festivity. An oil lamp may be used "in the case of the sanctuary lamp."[38] The *General Instruction of the Roman Missal* calls for two, four, or six candles to be placed "next to the altar" and a seventh candle may be used when the Bishop celebrates the liturgy.[39] In some places candles are placed near the ambo or candle-bearers accompany the Gospel procession to the ambo.

Questions from Parishioners

Members of the liturgy committee might field questions from parishioners. The following are common questions relating to broader theological and liturgical issues the liturgy committee might reflect upon.

> 1. *As a member of the liturgy committee, I often have to listen to complaints from parishioners or questions and requests that seem really unreasonable and petty. It can be very annoying. How should I deal with these situations?*

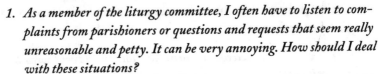

Members of the parish liturgy committee may not always even agree among themselves on every matter related to the liturgy. However, since the liturgy is "the sacrament of unity,"[40] all members of the committee must strive to achieve this goal of the council. Likewise, members of the parish—particularly the consistent complainers—must feel like they are being listened to, and that their ideas, suggestions, and complaints will be received in a spirit of charity. Members of the parish who may have something to share could be invited to attend a liturgy committee meeting and be given 10 to 15 minutes for presentation and discussion of a particular issue. Remember, one of the primary roles of the liturgy committee is to provide ongoing catechesis for the members of the community. Perhaps you could find an acquaintance of the complainer(s) who then works with them to help the complainer(s) better understand the issue. Remember, charity is at the heart of all we do; be patient, and make sure the persons feel they have been listened to. Always pray for understanding, patience, and resolution.

2. *For several years we have been offering our parishioners Holy Communion from the cup. We continue to hear many of the same questions regarding fear of disease and the possible spread of germs. One of the participants in the RCIA process asked us recently why do so many people pass by the cup, and why do so many leave after Holy Communion.*

The Church has given us the privilege to share in both the living bread and saving cup of Christ. We have this opportunity to experience what Christ has to offer us in as full a way as possible. Some may pass by the cup due to alcoholism or other diseases. Over the past 30 years the bishops of Catholic, Episcopal, and Lutheran Churches have conducted studies in conjunction with the center for disease control and other national medical agencies concerning the spread of diseases when drinking from the common cup. There are no studies to suggest that disease can be spread by drinking from a common cup. Breathing the same air and shaking hands are more likely to pass on "bugs" than sharing from the Communion cup. Of course, if one is sick with a cold, flu, or other communicable disease, that person should not drink from the cup until they have fully recovered. Whatever the reason a person may refrain from sharing in the blood of Christ, ours is not to make a judgment.

3. *One of our parishioners cannot have wheat products due to health concerns. How can he or she receive Holy Communion?*

Many individuals have a disease called celiac sprue or some other gluten intolerance. These individuals suffer harm from varying levels of consumption of gluten. Gluten is a significant ingredient in wheat flour, the main ingredient of validly made hosts. A "bread" without any gluten is not allowed. There are, however, very low-gluten hosts that might be possible for the communicant. These hosts are available from the Congregation of Benedictine Sisters of Perpetual Adoration in Clyde, Missouri.[41]

A communicant who cannot receive even the low-gluten host may still receive the precious blood. As has been taught within the Church from her earliest days, in receiving one species one receives the whole Christ.[42] With permission of the ordinary, those who cannot tolerate alcohol may recieve Holy Communion from the cup under the form of *mustum*. A special cup may be prepred for them at any Mass.

4. *Many of our parishioners have friends and family in the armed services. They often wonder why the American flag has been removed from the sanctuary of the church. Should we be honoring our country, instead of pushing it aside? Other parishioners have inquired about displaying the Vatican flag as well.*

The Bishops' Committee on Divine Worship has in the past encouraged pastors not to place the flag within the sanctuary itself, in order to reserve that space for the altar, the ambo, and the presidential chair. Instead, the suggestion has been made that the American flag be placed outside the sanctuary, or in the vestibule of the Church together with a book of prayer requests. The true banner we follow is the cross of our Lord Jesus Christ. As the GIRM reminds us, "all furnishings and decorations should serve that celebration of the liturgy and the active participation of the faithful in worship; they should be "signs and symbols of heavenly realities."[43] The Church provides similar guidelines concerning flags at funerals. The *Order of Christian Funerals* (OCF) reminds us that the white pall serves as an extension of the baptismal garment given to a deceased person at his or her Baptism. Since the Mass of Christian Burial makes constant allusion to Baptism, the pall is retained at Mass. The OCF states: Only Christian symbols may rest on or be placed near the coffin during the funeral liturgy. Any other symbols, for example, national flags or flags or insignia of associations, "have no place in the funeral liturgy."[44] The honors paid by the nation to one of its soldiers or veterans (symbolized by the use of the American flag and, perhaps, other military honors) are more appropriately incorporated into the graveside rites. For more guidelines from the United States Bishops consult this Web site: www.usccb.org/liturgy/ q&a/flag.shtml.

As for the papal flag—it is not a symbol of the Catholic Church, but the official flag of the tiny nation of Vatican City State. Because it represents the Vatican as a political entity, rather than the Catholic

Church itself, its use should be governed by the same principles as the flag of any other nation.

To be sensitive to the needs of the assembly, a lovely alternative idea is to display the flag proudly in the narthex. Place flowers and book of prayer beside it. With the current status of world affairs, many parishioners will have loved ones and close friends who are serving in the military. Doing the aforementioned shows support for our members of the armed services while respecting the integrity of the worship space. You may contact your local Office for Divine Worship to request the position of the local Bishop.[45]

NOTES

1. See *Fulfilled in Your Hearing*, 106–108.

2. CSL, 19.

3. For example: *Constitution on the Sacred Liturgy, General Instruction of the Roman Missal, Lectionary for Mass: Introduction, Sing to the Lord: Music in Divine Worship, Built of Living Stones*, and others.

4. See CSL, 44–46.

5. CSL, 26.

6. As originally published in *The Liturgical Ministry Series: Guide for Ministers of the Liturgical Environment* (LTP, 2008) by Paul Turner and Mary Patricia Storms.

7. See 1 Thessalonians 5:17.

8. Available from GIA publications, Chicago, Illinois, www.giamusic.com.

9. Available from Oregon Catholic Press, Portland, Oregon, www.ocp.org.

10. Available from World Library Publications, Schiller Park, Illinois, www.wlp.jspaluch.com.

11. Available from The Liturgical Press, Collegeville, Minnesota, litpress.org.

12. Available from Liturgy Training Publications, Chicago, Illinois, www.LTP.org.

13. This question has been adapted from the original article, "Implementing the Liturgy of the Hours in the Parish" by Michael R. Prendergast. The article first appeared in *Rite* magazine, volume 39, number 1.

14. CSL, 14 (Vatican translation).

15. See CSL, 30.

16. GIRM, 45.

17. Ibid.

18. This question has been adapted from the original article, "The Role of Silence in Lenten Liturgies" by Anthony Ruff, OSB. The article first appeared in *Rite* magazine, volume 38, number 6.

19. See "Seven Gestures of Intercultural Hospitality" by Rufino Zaragoza, OFM. *Today's Liturgy* (Portland, OR: Oregon Catholic Press), Advent/Christmas/Epiphany, 2008, p. 28.

20. Francis, Mark. *Guidelines for Multicultural Celebrations* (Washington, DC: Federation of Diocesan Liturgical Commissions), 1998 as quoted in "Seven Gestures of Intercultural Hospitality" by Rufino Zaragoza, OFM. *Today's Liturgy* (Portland, OR: Oregon Catholic Press), Advent/Christmas/Epiphany, 2008, pg. 28.

21. Eucharist Prayer for Masses of Reconciliation II.

22. See GIRM, 73–74.

23. See GIRM, 85.

24. See BCL *Newsletter* Vol. XXV, May 1989.

25. CSL, 55.

26. GIRM, 85.

27. In *The Liturgical Ministry Series: Guide for Sacristans* (LTP, 2008), Corrina Laughlin recommends: "A good way to ensure that [there are enough hosts] is to count the actual number in the assembly before preparing the hosts for Mass. The ushers can often help with this. If you put out the same number of hosts as there are people in the assembly (and don't forget to count the choir and the other ministers) you will be sure to have enough for everyone.

   "If hosts do need to be brought from the tabernacle, a minister may do it during the Sign of Peace. The ciborium can be placed on the altar and the priest can add hosts to the ciboria as well as from the hosts consecrated during the Mass. This is necessary at times, especially if there are many latecomers who were not factored into the count! This is also a good way to ensure that the hosts that are reserved in the tabernacle are kept fresh. However, it's always a good rule of thumb to include a little extra. Latecomers will always arrive!"

28. See *Eucharisticum Mysterium*, 49; *Holy Communion and Worship of the Eucharist Outside Mass*, 5.

29. GIRM, 69. Visit www.LTP.org/prayer of the faithful for downloadable intercessions.

30. CSL, 106.

31. *Paschale Solemnitatis* (PS), 85.

32. Ibid.

33. *General Norms for the Liturgical Year and the Caldndar* (GNLYC), 21.

34. Ibid.

35. See also PS, 77–78.

36. See *Book of Blessings* (BB), ch. 47.

37. See BB, ch. 48.

38. *Holy Communion and Worship of the Eucharist Outside of Mass,* 11.

39. GIRM, 117.

40. CSL, 26.

41. This community of sisters can be reached by phone (1-800-223-2772) or via the Web (www.benedictinesisters.org/altarbread/orderform.html). For additional information concerning celiac sprue disease, see also the USCCB Web site (http://www.usccb.org/liturgy/celiasprue.shtml).

42. See GIRM, 282; *Norms for the Celebration and Reception of Holy Communion under Both Kinds in the Dioceses of the United States of America* (NDRHC), 15. This question was adapted from *The Liturgical Ministry Series: Guide for Extraordinary Ministers of Holy Communion* (LTP, 2008), p. 41.

43. GIRM, 349.

44. *Order of Christian Funerals* (OCF), 38.

45. This last paragraph provided by Jill Maria Murdy was originally published in *Sourcebook for Sundays and Seasons: An Almanac of Parish Liturgy 2008.*

Resources

Documents and Reference Books

Documents on the Liturgy, 1963 – 1979: Conciliar, Papal and Curial Texts. Collegeville, MN: The Liturgical Press, 1982. A compendium of documents on the liturgy flowing from the heals of the Second Vatican Council. The "General Index" is especially helpful for locating broad documentation on various topics concerning the liturgy.

Eucharistic Documents for the New Millennium: Documentos Eucaristicos para el Nuevo Milenio. Chicago, IL: Liturgy Training Publications, 2004. A companion to the *General Instruction of the Roman Missal*, containing documents in both English and Spanish that will greatly assist faith communities to prepare for and evaluate the community's celebration of the Lord's Day Eucharist. Included documents are *Ecclesia de Eucharistia* and *Redemptionis Sacramentum.*

Flannery, OP, Austin. *Vatican Council II: Constitutions, Decrees, Declarations.* Northport, NY: Costello Publishing Company, 1996. This inclusive language translation of all of the Council's constitutions, decrees, and declarations is a key resource for understanding the Church's fundamental teaching on liturgy, ecclesiology, ministry, ecumenism, and more. Also available from LTP.

Fink, Peter E., ed. *The New Dictionary of Sacramental Worship.* Collegeville, MN: The Liturgical Press/Michael Glazier, 1990. A fine dictionary of worship and sacraments containing solid theological and practical pastoral essays that are essential for a rich liturgical and sacramental Church.

The Liturgy Documents: A Parish Resource, Volume One, fourth edition. Chicago, IL: Liturgy Training Publications, 2004. A key resource of primary liturgical documents that belongs in every parish resource library. This volume includes the *General Instruction of the Roman Missal* and the *Lectionary for Mass: Introduction*.

The Liturgy Documents: A Parish Resource, Volume Two. Chicago, IL: Liturgy Training Publications, 1999. More Vatican and conference documents with a very helpful topical index for both volumes of this resource. The book includes over ten documents including *Dies Domini, Paschale Solemnitatis, General Instruction of the Liturgy of the Hours, Inculturation and the Roman Liturgy.*

Thirty-five Years of the BCL Newsletter (1965–2000). Bishops' Committee on the Liturgy, Washington, DC: United States Conference of Catholic Bishops, 2004. A hefty volume of unique and consistent insights into the reforms mandated by the Second Vatican Council.

Liturgical Theology

Driscoll, Jeremy. *What Happens at Mass.* Chicago, IL: Liturgy Training Publications, 2005. This Benedictine scholar and teacher of students, in both the United States and Rome, provides the reader with a journey through Mass by giving attention to what happens when we celebrate the sacred mysteries. Written in a style that is within the reach of the average member of the Sunday liturgical assembly.

Francis, Mark R. *Shape the Circle Ever Wider.* Chicago, IL: Liturgy Training Publications, 2000. A primer for exploring the subject of inculturation and how it interfaces with the liturgy. This resource offers practical guidance and new insights for serving the ever-changing face of the Church in North America.

Huels, John M. *Liturgy and Law: Liturgical Law in the System of Roman Catholic Cannon Law.* Montreal (Quebec), Canada: Wilson and Lafleur Ltee, 2006. A resource that provides a clear path for interpretating liturgical law. The book is filled with solid examples that will assist one in understanding the principles and rules of interpretation, the role of custom, permissions, faculties, dispensations, and other topics related to liturgical law.

Martin, Kenneth J. *The Forgotten Instruction: The Roman Liturgy, Inculturation, and Legitimate Adaptations.* Chicago, IL: Liturgy Training Publications, 2008. Explores the evolution of the Church's theology and practice of inculturation and describes how these insights have influenced the accommodations and adaptations made within the Roman liturgy.

Prendergast, Michael R., ed. *Full, Conscious and Active Participation: Celebrating Twenty-five Years of Today's Liturgy.* Portland, OR: Pastoral Press, 2003. A series of articles by today's best pastoral liturgists including J. Michael Joncas, Elaine Rendler, Paul Covino, and S. Linda Gaupin. The articles are on a broad range of topics including pastoral liturgy, liturgical music, rites, the liturgical year, and Eucharist. An excellent source of catechesis on the liturgy for both liturgy committees and members of the liturgical assembly.

Liturgical Preparation

Belford, William J., Glenn C.J. Byer, and Michael R. Prendergast. *Parish Liturgy Basics.* Portland, OR: Pastoral Press, 2005. This resource offers concise answers to over three hundred questions about liturgy, Mass, sacraments, liturgical ministers, devotions, and more. The list of supporting documentation for the answers to each question, coming from conciliar, papal curial, and conference documents, is a unique feature of this helpful resource.

Flemming, Austin, with Victoria M. Tufano. *Preparing for Liturgy: A Theology and Spirituality.* Chicago, IL: Liturgy Training Publications, 1997. We always prepare the liturgy, for the Church has already planned the liturgy. Discover the difference in this reputable book.

Huck, Gabe, and Gerald T. Chinchar. *Liturgy with Style and Grace.* Chicago, IL: Liturgy Training Publications, 1998. Here is a "how to" book for the parish liturgy committees and all who prepare the liturgy of the Church. This book contains short essays on Mass, sacraments, and the liturgical year, along with thoughtful reflection questions.

————. *The Three Days: Parish Prayer in the Paschal Triduum.* Liturgy Training Publications, 1992. A comprehensive resource to assist communities in preparing the liturgies of Holy Thursday, Good Friday, and the Easter Vigil, one liturgy that unfolds over three days.

Johnson, Lawrence J. *The Mystery of Faith: A Study of the Structural Elements of the Mass.* Washington, DC: Federation of Diocesan Liturgical Commissions, 2003. One of the finest catechetical resources on the Order of Mass. As you walk through the Mass you find a concise historical overview of each section of the Mass, supporting citations from both Vatican and U.S. documents, a brief summary, and helpful reflections questions.

Mazar, Peter. *To Crown the Year: Decorating the Church through the Seasons.* Chicago, IL: Liturgy Training Publications, 1995. Although dated, this "how to" workbook is for all who ready the church for ritual prayer. The book walks one through the liturgical seasons and provides creative thoughts and ideas for representing appropriate decor for each season while linking the whole year together.

Pastoral Liturgy® (formerly *Rite*). Chicago, IL: Liturgy Training Publications. This journal, published six times a year, delves into the pastoral nature of liturgy and aids in the preparation of liturgy, the catechesis of children and youth, the spiritual development of its readers, and adds to their knowledge of the historical development of the liturgy.

Turner, Paul. *A Guide to the General Instruction of the Roman Missal.* Chicago, IL: Liturgy Training Publications, 2003. A brief, handy guide with a straightforward commentary on the *General Instruction of the Roman Missal* for ordained and lay ecclesial ministers. Turner, not only a scholar but a fine pastor, highlights three important principles: the sacrifice of Christ, the holiness of Eucharist, and the participation of the ministers.

Various authors. *Sourcebook for Sundays, Seasons, and Weekdays: The Almanac for Pastoral Liturgy.* Chicago, IL: LTP. A detailed, day-to-day handbook to accompany those who prepare the liturgy. Includes notes on the Lectionary and Roman Missal and suggestions for celebrating feasts and seasons in the domestic Church. Published annually.

Ritual Texts

Note: Each of the rituals of the Roman rite has its own ritual book. Several of these texts appear in study editions. It is important that parish liturgy committees have access to these texts when preparing the various celebrations of the rites and sacraments in the parish community. Here is a list of the Roman Catholic ritual books:

- *Book of Blessings*
- *Lectionary for Mass (Sunday, Weekday, and Ritual Masses)*
- *Lectionary for Masses with Children*
- *Liturgy of the Hours*
- *Order of Christian Funerals*
- *Order of Solemn Exposition*
- *Pastoral Care of the Sick: Rites of Anointing and Viaticum*
- *Rite of Baptism for Children*
- *Rite of Christian Initiation of Adults*
- *Rite of Confirmation*
- *Rite of Marriage*
- *Rite of Ordination*
- *Rite of Penance*
- *Roman Missal* (Sacramentary)
- *Sacramentary Supplement*
- *Sunday Celebrations in the Absence of a Priest*

Training Materials for Liturgical Ministers

Various authors. *The Liturgical Ministry Series.* Chicago, IL: Liturgy Training Publications.

These booklets provide the essential training materials and spiritual formation for all of your liturgical ministers. Written in warm and inviting tone by liturgical, theological, and pastoral ministry experts, these books include a theology and historical overview of the particular ministries, spiritual guidance, and the practical aspects of the minister's liturgical role and duties. Booklets currently in the series are *Guide for Cantors, Guide for Extraordinary Ministers of Holy Communion, Guide for Lectors, Guide for Music Ministers, Guide for Ministers of the Liturgical Environment, Guide for Sacristans, Guide for Servers,* and *Guide for Ushers and Greeters.*

Prayer and Reflection Resources

Various authors. *At Home with the Word.* Chicago, IL: LTP. This guide (published annually) offers a deeper understanding of all the Sunday readings for the liturgical year. It also offers insights into the readings from scripture scholars, and it suggests ways to practice the theological virtues of faith, hope, and charity. With prayers to begin and end your scripture reading, this is a great way for members of the liturgy committee to gain a better understanding of the Sunday scriptures for liturgical preparation.

Various authors. *Daily Prayer.* Chicago, IL: LTP. A must-have prayer resource for all liturgical ministers. Using a familiar order of prayer (psalmody, scripture, brief reflection, Prayer of the Faithful, Lord's Prayer, and closing prayer), this annual publication is ideal for personal and communal reflection upon the word of God. The portable size of this book makes it convenient to carry in a purse, briefcase, or backpack, and it provides an easy way to get into the habit of daily prayer that is in sync with the liturgical year. Published annually.

Web Resources

1. **Canadian Conference of Catholic Bishops (CCCB)**
   The CCCB is the national assembly of the Bishops of Canada. Its Web site contains links to documents and publications that serve the liturgy: **www.cccb.ca.**

2. **The Center for Liturgy at Saint Louis University**
   The Center for Liturgy at Saint Louis University exists to study and promote the celebration of the Mass and other liturgical rituals. Learn more at **www.liturgy.slu.edu.**

3. **Creighton University**
   A Web site that offers a mater-of-fact channel to a non-thematic method for liturgy preparation: **www.people.creighton.edu/ ~roc69903/.**

4. **Federation of Diocesan Liturgical Commissions (FDLC)**
   A national organization of liturgical leaders in each local Church that assists the local ordinary with the oversight of liturgy in each diocese. The FDLC serves as the representative collaborating instrument between the local Churches through diocesan worship offices and liturgical commissions and the USCCB Bishops' Committee on Divine Worship. Their Web site: **www. fdlc.org.**

5. **Georgetown Center for Liturgy**

   The center's mission is the work for transforming a church through a renewed liturgy by providing adequate sources and activities to engage the church at the parish, diocesan, regional and national levels. Its new online community, Envision Church, reports the latest design in church architecture and environment that allows members to interact with this attractive and formative Web site: **http://centerforliturgy.georgetown.edu/**.

6. **GIA Publications, Inc.**

   GIA's online resources include copyright licensees for several publishers, music engravings, and liturgy preparation resources. Their Web sites: **www.giamusic.com; www.OneLicense.net; www.HymnPrint.net; www.LiturgyHelp.com**.

7. **Liturgy Training Publications**

   Visit this site for a **free** download of additional resources for all aspects of liturgy. Originally published in *Sourcebook for Sundays, Seasons, and Weekdays,* this list of resources is updated each year and is available as a PDF. LTP's Web site: **www.LTP.org**.

8. **National Association of Pastoral Musicians** (NPM)

   A member organization that nurtures the art of musical liturgy. The members of NPM serve the Catholic Church in the United States and beyond as musicians, clergy, liturgists, and leaders of ritual prayer. Their Web site: **www.npm.org**.

9. **Notre Dame Center for Liturgy**

   A center dedicated to liturgical research and pastoral liturgy. The center sponsors an online liturgy network, an annual summer conference. It also publishes books and other resources. Their Web site: **www.liturgy.nd.edu**.

10. **Oregon Catholic Press (OCP)**

    OCP maintains Web sites in support of churches with resources of music engravings and a custom worship program maker, online licensees for several music publishers, and a liturgy preparation tool. All these resources work together to form a comprehensive support system for ministry. Their Web sites: **www.ocp.org; www.liturgy.com; www.printandpraise.com; www.spiritandsong.com.**

11. **United States Conference of Catholic Bishops (USCCB)**
The Web site of the U.S. Bishops contains links to liturgical resources and documents. Here you will also find links to the *New American Bible*, the readings from the *Lectionary for Mass* and podcasts of the day's readings. Their Web site: **www.usccb. org**. The Committee on Divine Worship of the USCCB provides excellent resources on their site as well: **www.usccb.org/ liturgy/divworsecretariat.shtml**.

Glossary

ADVENT: The first season of the liturgical year, beginning four Sundays before Christmas and ending after Midafternoon Prayer on Christmas Eve. The name means "coming." During Advent we wait joyfully for the Second Coming of the Lord at the end of time and also to his birth at Christmas.

AMBO: A Greek word that means "a raised platform or reading desk." It is often referred to as the pulpit or lectern and is the place from where the Sacred Scriptures—including the Responsorial Psalm—the homily, and the Prayer of the Faithful are read or chanted during the liturgy.

AMBRY: Repository for the oil of catechumens, oil of the sick, and sacred chrism.

APOSTOLIC SEE: The Episcopal See of Rome. The Pope as Bishop of Rome has supreme authority over the regulation of the liturgy. Also called the Holy See.

ASSEMBLY: All those who gather for liturgical worship make up the assembly, the Body of Christ, the Church. The assembly is ordered hierarchically, arranged by rank and function.

BISHOPS' COMMITTEE ON DIVINE WORSHIP (BCDW): Formerly the Bishops' Committee on the Liturgy (BCL), this committee of the United States Bishops oversees the liturgy for all dioceses of the United States. They publish a monthly newsletter for pastoral use.

BOOK OF THE GOSPELS: A ritual book that contains the Gospel passages for Sundays, solemnities, and feasts of the Lord. It is used by a deacon, or in his absence, a priest, to proclaim the Gospel during liturgy. The Book of the Gospels is venerated, always with a kiss and sometimes with incense, since "Christ himself is present . . . through his word."[1]

CELIAC SPRUE: A disease afflicting persons, at varying levels of tolerance, who cannot ingest wheat gluten without becoming ill.

CHRISTMAS: Begins with Evening Prayer on Christmas Eve and ends with Evening Prayer on the feast of the Baptism of the Lord. It is the season of the Incarnation.

COMMISSIONED: This term refers to a public act of installing and blessing a member of the laity into ministries of service not requiring ordination for either single or multiple occasions.

CONCLUDING RITE: The end of Mass following the Prayer after Communion. At this time, any necessary announcements are heard, the Final Blessing is given, and the assembly is dismissed, transformed by the word they have heard and the Eucharist they have received, "to love and serve the Lord."[2]

CONFERENCE OF BISHOPS: Made up of of all bishops of a particular country or locale. The mission of the bishops of the United States is to "act collaboratively and consistently on vital issues confronting the Church and society; foster communion with the Church in other nations, within the Church universal, under the leadership of its supreme pastor, the Roman Pontiff; and offer appropriate assistance to each bishop in fulfilling his particular ministry in the local Church."[3]

DEVOTIONS: Prayers or private acts of worship. The *Constitution on the Sacred Liturgy* reminds us that devotions should "harmonize with the liturgical seasons, accord with the sacred liturgy, are in some way derived from it, and lead the people to it, since, in fact, the liturgy, by its very nature far surpasses any of them."[4]

EASTER: Begins on Easter Sunday and ends with Evening Prayer on the solemnity of Pentecost. It is the 50-day celebration of Christ's Resurrection, Ascension into heaven, and the sending of the Holy Spirit.

FEAST: Second ranking of liturgical observances of the Lord and of the saints. These days are confined only to the natural day; that is, they do not have a vigil and do not begin the evening before. *See also memorial and solemnity.*

INDULT: A concession or favor granted by the lawful superior (Pope, Apostolic See, Bishop) that allows the recipient to do something that the common law of the Church does not always permit. Indults from recent decades include allowing the cremated remains to be present at a funeral Mass, allowing bishops providing permission to seminarians to preach at Mass during a parish internship prior to their ordination to the diaconate, or the permission to receive Holy Communion in the hand.

INTERNATIONAL COMMISSION ON ENGLISH IN THE LITURGY (ICEL): "A mixed commission of Catholic Bishops' Conferences in countries where English is used in the celebration of the Sacred Liturgy according to the Roman rite. The purpose of the Commission is to prepare English translations of each of the Latin liturgical books and any individual liturgical texts in accord with the directives of the Holy See."[5]

INTRODUCTORY RITE: The purpose of this rite "is to ensure that the faithful who come together as one establish communion and dispose themselves to listen properly to God's word and celebrate the Eucharist worthily."[6] It consists of the Entrance Procession and Song, Sign of the Cross, Opening Greeting, Penitential Act (Penitential Rite), Kyrie, Rite of Blessing and Sprinkling Holy Water, Gloria, and Collect (Opening Prayer).

LECTIONARY FOR MASS: The word *lectionary* comes from the Latin word for reading—*lectio*. The *Lectionary for Mass* contains a collection of scripture readings appointed for Catholic worship on a given day or occasion.

LENT: Begins on Ash Wednesday and ends with the celebration of the Evening Mass of the Lord's Supper on Holy Thursday. It is a penitential season, preparing those for the celebration of Baptism and the renewal of baptismal promises at Easter.

LITURGICAL YEAR: "Christ's saving work is celebrated in sacred memory by the Church on fixed days throughout the year. Each week on the day called the Lord's Day the Church commemorates the Lord's resurrection. Once a year at Easter the Church honors this resurrection and passion with the utmost solemnity. In fact through the yearly cycle the Church unfolds the entire mystery of Christ and keeps the anniversary of the saints."[7]

LITURGY: From the Greek *leitourgia*, originally meaning "a public act" (the "work of the people") performed for the good of the community. In the Roman Catholic Church, the word is used in reference to any of the official rites of the Church as found in the Roman ritual book. This would include, for example, Mass, the Liturgy of the Hours, word services, and celebrations of the sacraments. Liturgy is always worship of God the Father, through Christ in the power of the Holy Spirit. It is a celebration of the Paschal Mystery of Jesus Christ in which our salvation is accomplished—the source of our life and a journey toward the heavenly banquet.

LITURGY COMMITTEE: A team of people with varying expertise and skills who help prepare a community to carry out the Church's plan of worship.

LITURGY OF THE EUCHARIST: The part of the Mass that follows the Prayer of the Faithful and concludes with the Prayer after Communion. The structure follows a fourfold Biblically based format: take, bless, break, and share. We begin with the Preparation of the Gifts, the bread and the wine (taking), the praying of the Eucharistic Prayer (blessing), followed by the Lord's Prayer and Sign of Peace. During the chanting of the Lamb of God, the bread is broken (breaking), and then we partake of the sacred elements (sharing) during Holy Communion. The Liturgy of the Word and the Liturgy of the Eucharist form but "one single act of worship."[8]

LITURGY OF THE HOURS: The official prayer of the Church that shapes and sanctifies each day. The Psalter, or book of the Psalms, is by tradition the heart of the Liturgy of the Hours. It is sometimes referred to as the Divine Office.

LITURGY OF THE WORD: The section of the Mass or ritual that follows the Introductory Rite. The liturgy may include several readings from scripture followed by a homily, Profession of Faith (if prescribed), and the Prayer of the Faithful. On Sundays and major feasts of the liturgical year, three readings are prescribed, while at a weekday celebration, only two. The readings always follow this order: First Reading, Responsorial Psalm, Second Reading (Sequence on Easter and Pentecost), Acclamation before the Gospel, and Gospel.

MEMORIAL: The third ranking of celebrations of the saints. They are either obligatory (that is, they must be celebrated) or optional. *See also feast and solemnity.*

NAVE: The main section of the church building. The nave may contain pews or chairs for the people and is usually distinct from the sanctuary area.

ORDO: Book or leaflet, published locally or regionally, giving detailed information about each day of the liturgical year.

ORDINARY TIME: Begins after Evening Prayer on the feast of the Baptism of the Lord until Ash Wednesday, and from after Evening Prayer I on the solemnity of Pentecost until Evening Prayer of the First Sunday of Advent. *Ordinary* comes from the word *ordinal* and means "counted." In other words, each of the weeks has a number (for example, the *Third* Sunday in Ordinary Time). There are 33 or 34 weeks of Ordinary Time, which is full of solemnities, feasts, and memorials of the Lord and the saints.

PARISH/PASTORAL COUNCIL: In accord with canon 536 of the Code of Canon Law, a parish pastoral council is to be established in each parish or cluster of parishes. It is a collaborative body of the Christian faithful whose purpose is the promotion of the mission of Jesus Christ and the Church. The liturgy committee flows from this council.

PASCHAL TRIDUUM: Begins on Holy Thursday with the Evening Mass of the Lord's Supper and ends with Evening Prayer on Easter Sunday. *Triduum* means the "Three Days of Passover." During this short season, the followers of Jesus proclaim that in the life, Passion, death, and Resurrection of Jesus, God has freed and saved us. This is the high point of the entire liturgical year.

PROMULGATE: The formal implementation of a Church document or ritual.

RITUAL: The word *ritual* comes from the Latin *ritualis*, meaning "rite" or "form." Ritual can be described as the prescribed words and actions of a liturgical function.

RITUAL BOOKS: Official text for Roman Catholic worship. Liturgical or ritual books include the *praenotanda* (pastoral introduction to the rite) and the ritual text with rubrics (directions). The original text is in Latin but is translated into the vernacular.

RITUAL GESTURE: Movements by the body of Christ or the presiding minister during the liturgy. These would include *orans* (arms outstretched), laying on of hands, kissing of altar or Book of the Gospels, genuflections, and bows.

ROMAN MISSAL: The Roman Missal, from the Latin *Missale Romanum*, is the liturgical book containing the texts and rubrics for the celebration of the Mass in the Roman rite. Also referred to as the Sacramentary.

SACRAMENT: A basic definition of sacraments that has served people well for generations is "an outward sign instituted by Christ to give grace."[9] Since sacraments are not private events, they can be seen as actions of Christ and the Church.

SACRAMENTALS: "Sacred signs by which effects, especially spiritual effects, are signified in some imitation of the sacraments and are obtained through the intercession of the Church."[10] Common objects and actions considered sacramentals are blessed objects, palms, holy water, and blessings.

SACRED CONGREGATION FOR DIVINE WORSHIP AND THE DISCIPLINE OF THE SACRAMENTS: A dicastery or department in the Roman Curia responsible for the liturgical life of the universal Roman Catholic Church.

SANCTORAL CYCLE: The observances of Mary and the saints during the liturgical year. Most occur on fixed dates and are ranked as solemnity, feast, or memorial (obligatory or optional). *See also temporal cycle.*

SANCTUARY: The area of the church building in which the presidential chair, altar, and ambo are located. Most sanctuaries are elevated for the sake of visibility. This area is sometimes referred to as the presbyterium or chancel.

SOLEMNITY: The highest rank of a liturgical observance. These celebrations include not only the day itself, but also the evening before, beginning with either Evening Prayer or with a vigil Mass. *See also feast and memorial.*

SUNDAY: The most important day of the Christian week. "In the weekly reckoning of time Sunday recalls the day of Christ's resurrection. It is *Easter* which returns week by week, celebrating Christ's victory over sin and death, the fulfillment in him of the first creation and the dawn of 'the new creation' (cf. 2 Corinthians 5:17). It is the day which recalls in grateful adoration the world's first day and looks forward in active hope to 'the last day,' when Christ will come in glory (cf. Acts 1:11; 1 Thessalonians 4:13–17) and all things will be made new (cf. Revelation 21:5)."[11]

TEMPORAL CYCLE: The seasons throughout the liturgical year. The high seasons are Advent, Christmas, Lent, Paschal Triduum, and Easter. The remaining time is Ordinary Time. *See also sanctoral cycle.*

VERNACULAR: Language proper to a particular country or locale.

VOX CLARA: Latin for "clear voice," Vox Clara is a consultative committee of bishops, priests, and other consultants, established in 2002 by Pope John Paul II to assist the Sacred Congregation for Divine Worship and Discipline of the Sacraments in fulfilling its responsibilities with regard to the English translations of the Latin liturgical texts.

NOTES

1. GIRM, 55.

2. *Roman Missal*, Concluding Rite.

3. www.usccb.org.

4. CSL, 13.

5. www.icelweb.org.

6. GIRM, 46.

7. GNLYC, 1.

8. CSL, 56.

9. Traditional definition from the *Baltimore Catechism*.

10. *Code of Canon Law*, §1166.

11. *Dies Domini*, 1.

Appendix I

Sample Liturgy Committee Agenda

1. Prayer (5 min.)
Based on the season we are in or about to prepare for.

2. Short catechesis (15–20 min.)
Study of liturgical documents or discussion of an article or section of a book read ahead of time by all the members.

3. Review last meeting's minutes (5 min.)
Corrections of minutes that were in the hands of all committee members at least one week before this meeting.

4. Review agenda (2 min.)
Are there any agenda additions?

5. Pending (5 min.)
Review any unresolved issues or work of the committee not yet completed.

6. Evaluation of previous season (15–20 min.)
Key issues concerning hospitality, liturgical art and environment, ritual, music.

7. Liturgical ministers (5 min.)
Any attention needed to presiders, deacons, preaching, music minister, lectors, sacristans, ministers of hospitality, ushers, servers, and others?

8. Key issues regarding upcoming season(s) (15–20 min.)
Hospitality, liturgical art and environment, ritual, music, other?

9. Review timeline for tasks and jobs to be completed (5 min.)

10. Closing prayer (2 min.)

Michael R. Prendergast © 2009 Archdiocese of Chicago: Liturgy Training Publications, 3949 South Racine Avenue, Chicago IL 60609; 1-800-933-1800; www.LTP.org.

Appendix II

Liturgy Evaluation Form

This form can be adapted for the various seasons (Advent/Christmas; Ordinary Time during winter; Lent/Triduum/Easter; Ordinary Time during summer and fall).

Hospitality

1. What special efforts were made to invite and welcome visitors (in the broadest sense of the word) to your community during these seasons?

    _____

    _____

    _____

    _____

2. What positive effort was made to invite them to return soon and often?

    _____

    _____

    _____

    _____

Liturgical Art and Environment

1. How did the decor of your worship space support the sacredness of the liturgy and each rite during the season?

_____

_____

_____

_____

2. How did the decor enhance your experience of assembly, worship, and prayer?

_____

_____

_____

_____

3. Were the materials used for the sacramentals (e.g., ashes, palms, oils, basin and towels, cross, Easter fire, Paschal candle, assembly candles, candles for the newly baptized, baptismal water, Eucharistic bread and wine) inspiring visually?

_____

_____

_____

_____

4. Were all of the symbols used in the liturgy honest and robust, pointing to the immanence and transcendence of God?

_____

_____

_____

_____

Ritual

1. Which rituals seem to flow naturally? Why do you think so?

_____

_____

_____

_____

2. Which rites felt "long" or "disconnected?" Why?

_____

_____

_____

_____

3. Did the rituals speak of sacredness, mystery, beauty, and noble simplicity?

_____

_____

_____

_____

Liturgical Music

1. Did the lyrics of hymns and songs express the meaning of each rite they accompanied?

_____

_____

_____

2. Were most tunes familiar to the assembly?

_____

_____

_____

_____

3. Did the music for the assembly allow for full participation? How?

_____

_____

_____

_____

4. Did music used during the special rites of each (acclamations, litanies, etc.) involve the assembly's response to the sacramental actions taking place?

_____

_____

_____

_____

5. Was the music wedded to the ritual movements (e.g., processions, special rituals, and bread breaking)?

_____

_____

_____

_____

Special Rituals

1. What other liturgies did you celebrate in this season (e.g., Liturgy of the Hours, RCIA, communal Penance, communal Anointing of the Sick, blessings)?

_____

_____

_____

_____

2. Evaluate each of the above in terms of hospitality, environment, ritual, and music.

_____

_____

_____

_____

Considerations

1. What did we do well?

_____

_____

_____

_____

2. What needs more attention or is in need of change for next
   year?

   _____

   _____

   _____

   _____

3. Are there any needs that will require budgetary or staff adjustments or changes?

   _____

   _____

   _____

   _____

Appendix III

Discernment Process

The Roman Catholic Diocese of Brooklyn, New York, Office of Pastoral Planning, contains rich information for leading a group through a discernment process for a creating a parish pastoral council. Several PDFs are available as a free download. These include processes for discernment and prayer services and can be adapted for use when forming a parish liturgy committee: http://pastoralplanning.diobrook.org/pastoral-planning/parish/parish-pastoral-councils/discernment-process/.

The following book contains worksheets and a process for discernment: *Revisioning the Parish Pastoral Council* by Mary Ann Gubish, Susan Jenny, Arlene McGannon. Paulist Press, 2001.

O God, you have gathered us together,
   as Moses gathered the chosen people,
   and as Jesus gathered his disciples.
We stand in awe at the call you have made,
   bidding us to serve your Church at prayer.
Make us mindful of your sacred mysteries
   and help us celebrate them in spirit and truth.
We ask this through Christ our Lord.
Amen.

Notes

Notes

Notes

Notes
